INDIAN
& MALAY
ETIQUETTE

INDIAN
& MALAY
ETIQUETTE
A Matter of Course

Raelene Tan

LANDMARK BOOKS PTE LTD
5001, Beach Road, #02-73/74, Singapore 0719

ISBN 981-3002-58-1

Films processed by Superskill Graphics Pte Ltd
Printed by Loi Printing Pte Ltd

TABLE OF CONTENTS

Author's Preface   7

Indian Etiquette   11

Gifts and Occasions   26

Dining Etiquette   37

Table Etiquette   47

Festive Fare   59

Food, Glorious Food!   62

≈

Malay Etiquette   67

Gifts and Occasions   79

Dining Etiquette   86

Table Etiquette   93

Festive Fare   103

Food, Glorious Food!   107

Index   110

ACKNOWLEDGEMENTS

*My patient husband and children deserve
kudos for putting up with my long and erratic
hours of research.*

*Others who deserve special thanks for their
invaluable assistance are Mr S.V. Krishnan,
Ms Anita Mohamad, Ms Prema Muthucumaru,
Mr Bhajan Singh, Ms Dhershini Winodan
and all those persons whose table manners
I observed without their realising.*

AUTHOR'S PREFACE

When I was approached to write a series of books on table etiquette, I had no idea that it would be such an immense task – enjoyable but daunting.

Indian and Malay Etiquette – A Matter of Course has been written as a guide to food etiquette and is not meant to be a guide to customs and traditions.

With some knowledge of what lies behind a particular occasion, whether it be a visit to a friend's home, a wedding reception or a business gathering, it is bound to be more enjoyable. Table etiquette alone, I feel, is not sufficient. That is why special occasions have been mentioned in this book.

Important common factors among various Asian communities include the removing of shoes before entering homes, the using of the right hand, modesty of dress and significance of colours and numbers. Because they are not usual practices for many non-Asians, they have been touched on here.

Blunders cover such matters as Western-ers unwittingly ordering and eating individual dishes of Asian food, as they would Western dishes, to other ethnic persons sharing food from central serving dishes using their individual cutlery.

Almost any awkward situation can be resolved, simply by making a little joke against oneself, or simply eating humble pie and apologising sincerely.

Here are some bits to chew on.

It is better to plead ignorance than to offend. No one will get upset when you humbly mention beforehand that you do not know something.

Ask and you will be told. Others are usually willing to help and show what they know.

If you cannot ask, then watch. Copy the actions of someone who knows what to do.

Having manners simply means being thoughtful towards others, and showing respect and tolerance. If we are considerate in our attitude, we can never offend or hurt others.

The aim of this book, therefore, is to make cross-cultural interaction, especially at social occasions, even more pleasurable. It is also for people in business who entertain clients from different cultural backgrounds.

Without help and encouragement from my friends, this book could not have been completed. I asked so many questions, they patiently replied, cooked and demonstrated and asked me questions in return. I wrangled invitations to wedding ceremonies and receptions, homes, restaurants and business gatherings, to prod, pry and question. Not only did my knowledge increase, but also my weight!

It must be said here that this is not a book of strict rules. It is simply my hope that *Indian and Malay Etiquette – A Matter of Course* helps to answer questions on the table and social etiquette of these two cultures.

Raelene Tan
1992

INDIAN ETIQUETTE

Indians are known for their gentle, colourful and diverse life styles and for their cultural heritage in the arts and food.

As a people, they belong to several different faiths. Hindus form the largest religious group and there are also Sikhs, Buddhists, Muslims and Christians, among others.

The people of the different religions and sects observe different customs and traditions. It is difficult therefore to state categorically the pertinent etiquette as appropriate to Indian manners. However, the information in this book takes into account the most common traditions and is adequate for most social situations involving etiquette Indian style.

The Hindu religion is a way of life. Hindus believe in the ultimate reality, who appears in many forms for different purposes such as life, creation, energy, protection.

Reincarnation is believed in, in that one's life and actions will determine his next life, and that the actions of his previous life have determined his present life.

All Hindus are generally vegetarian, but ways have changed from the old traditions.

HINDU CALENDAR

The Hindu Indian calendar is based on the moon and begins the year in the month of April.

SIKHISM

Sikhism is a religion that originated in the Punjab, northwest India, at the beginning of the sixteenth century with Guru Nanak, and which incorporates Hindu and Muslim beliefs. (*Sikh* means 'disciple').

Sikhs are monotheists and strive to lead life according to the words of the holy book Sri Guru Granth Sahib. The five symbols of the religion are uncut and unshaven hair *(Kesa)* referring to saintliness; a comb *(Kangha)* signifying cleanliness; a steel bracelet *(Kara)* symbolising honesty and protection from evil, worn on the right arm; a double-edged sword *(Kirpan)* as an emblem of courage – these days in miniature form and often worn under the turban or around the neck – and special underwear *(Kacch)* to remind one to practise strict moral behaviour.

Male Sikhs are required to wear turbans on their heads and keep beards.

Sikhs observe their festivals by performing ceremonies in *gurdwara* (Sikh places of worship). The festivals include birthdays and other significant days in the lives of the Gurus, and the Sikh new year on 13 April.

SIKH CALENDAR

The Buddhist, Islamic and Christian religions have been embraced by some Indians and their beliefs are similar to those of the same religions as practised by other ethnic groups.

GREETINGS

If you wish to greet, or take leave of, an Indian person, the expression, *"Vanakkam"* or, *"Namaste"*, is appropriate. This is said with a smile and with the traditional gesture of placing both palms together at chest level and nodding the head gently once. This signifies two hearts together in friendship.

These days, shaking hands is often done, especially with foreigners. However, when greeting an Indian lady, it is best to let her make the first move. If she proffers her hand, then go ahead and shake hands. If she does not, then a smile and a simple nod of the head would be in order for both parties.

13

NAMES

Many Indians do not have surnames, as such, and this can be confusing for the non-Indian. Often the initial of their father is placed in front of their own name, such as A. Sivam — 'A' is the initial of the father's name (say, Arul) and Sivam is the person's own name. He could safely be addressed as Mr. Sivam. An Indian woman usually takes her husband's name upon marriage, so from being Miss R. Devi ('R' being the initial of her father's name), she becomes, upon marrying Mr A. Sivam, Mrs Sivam Devi, commonly addressed as Mrs Sivam. As can be seen, names only carry on for one generation.

Where there are two initials before the person's own name, as in A. P. Krishna, it could either be that the father was given two names or the person has two names. Commonly, only one name is used.

Sikhs have the suffix *'Singh'* (lion) for males and *'Kaur'* (princess) for females added to their names. For instance, Joginder Singh s/o (son of) Balwant Singh, would be addressed as Mr. Joginder Singh. Similarly Jaspal Kaur d/o (daughter of) Harbans Singh, married to Joginder Singh, would be addressed, in the main, as Mrs Joginder Singh, although she can still be correctly called Jaspal Kaur.

INTRODUCTIONS

In the Indian way, the older or most respected person's name is mentioned first when introducing people. A woman's name is mentioned before a gentleman's name when introducing the two. As in other Asian communities, 'Aunty' or 'Uncle' is the usual form of address for older persons even though there is no relationship. This is simply a form of respect.

FORM OF ADDRESS FOR OLDER PERSONS

Indian family members should be greeted according to age, beginning with the oldest.

VISITING AN INDIAN HOME

Most Indians are informal and enjoy inviting friends to their homes.

VISITING

Before entering a traditional Indian home, it is customary to remove your shoes and leave them at the door, but not blocking the entrance. If the host insists that shoes are worn indoors, they are never worn in the kitchen or in an area reserved for prayers.

REMOVAL OF SHOES

I remember well one Indian friend (a hospitable and highly educated gentleman) placing a sign at his front door whenever he entertained more than just a few friends (his wife is non-Indian), stating "My house is my Temple". Aside from cleanliness, he had beautiful hand-made carpets on his floor.

The entrance doorway to a Hindu home normally has a picture of a deity or two and a string of mango leaves at the top, symbolising the need for purity, and by the elongated shape of the leaves to remind one of the need for a sharpness of knowledge.

HINDU HOME DECOR

They also remind the family within to treat all persons well. These leaves are changed on festive days and other special occasions.

There is usually an area set apart for daily prayers, where statues or pictures of Hindu deities may be seen. A free-standing oil-lamp and perfumed incense are normally lit before prayers.

An intricate floral pattern *(rangoli)* on the floor or ground outside the entrance also indicates a Hindu household. The pattern is made using rice flour and it represents the intricacies of life joining together and forming a complete and beautiful picture. Rice flour is used as it is intended to feed birds and insects.

SIKH HOME DECOR

At the entrance to a Sikh household there is often a *khanda*, comprising two crossed swords shielding a circle and a light. One sword represents the strength of goodness and the other sword represents the strength to fight off evil. The life cycle is symbolised by the circle and the light signifies the divine. The *khanda* may be in picture form or made of brass. A Sikh home may have a room set aside for prayers, where the holy book Sri Guru Granth Sahib is kept.

An Indian Muslim home has a prayer rug on the floor and care should be taken by a guest not to stand or sit on the prayer rug. Also, a guest must not touch the Koran (holy book) without first asking permission.

MUSLIM PRAYER ITEMS

Muslims are not permitted to touch dogs, and if an Indian Muslim visits you and you own a dog, it would be best to keep your dog out of sight. Some Indians, also, prefer not to touch dogs and cats, so one should be sensitive to guests' feelings.

DOGS

If you are visiting an Indian home for the first time, be sure it is not a Thursday as superstition has it that the friendship will not last if the first visit is made on a Thursday. However, superstitions (and days) vary, so do check with your host before you call in for that first visit.

FIRST VISIT

It is often the host who greets guests upon their arrival, with the hostess remaining indoors.

If the wife of the host does not join you, it is simply that this is part of her upbringing. On the other hand, the men may congregate together and the women elsewhere. You will simply have to adapt to the ways of your Indian hosts.

SEATING

SEATING

Do not sit until your Indian host invites you to do so.

In a traditional Indian home, you may find yourself seated on mats or cushions on the floor. Men usually sit cross-legged, while women place their legs together to either side, with feet tucked away. When seated on a chair, it is best not to cross one leg over the other and not to expose the soles of one's shoes or feet as an act of courtesy. It is also impolite to swing one's legs.

WHEN OFFERED A DRINK

Even if you call unexpectedly on an Indian household, you will almost certainly be served with a drink. It is polite to drink all.

When an older person enters the room, it is usual to rise. Always remember to greet older people ('Aunty' or 'Uncle'), even without an introduction.

Take note that if you admire or praise a person or his possessions to extremes, it is believed that the Evil Eye will be attracted, so do be careful with your compliments.

SMOKING

To refrain from smoking would be extremely wise as traditional Indians consider the flame to be sacred.

USE OF LEFT HAND CONSIDERED TABOO

Do not use your left hand for any occasion as it is not considered proper by the Indian community.

When giving or receiving an item, the right hand must be used, supported by the left hand if necessary.

BODY-TOUCHING

Also, refrain from body-touching as this is

18

frowned upon by Indians. Caucasians, in particular, are a 'touching' people and should be aware of this point of etiquette. In particular, heads should not be touched. This applies to both children and adults alike.

If you wish to point in the presence of Indians, extend your right hand straight out without a waving motion, fingers and thumb outstretched together and the palm facing to the left. To use the index finger to point is ill-mannered. Pointing is sometimes done with the chin. To beckon, you gently wave your right hand, fingers downwards and palm towards your body, with fingers outstretched but together.

When passing in front of an Indian person, or persons, it is polite to bow slightly whilst walking and say, "Excuse me, please."

Often an Indian gives a shake of his, or her, head when he or she means "yes", so do clarify if you are unsure.

When taking leave of an Indian family, it is polite to approach all persons present in the house. It is not usual to say goodbye, but rather utter the words, "I'll go and come back," to which the reply will be, "Yes, go and come back."

Guests should stagger their departure a little and not leave *en masse*, even if you are of the same party, so as not to cause a sudden void.

POINTING

BECKONING

WHEN PASSING IN FRONT OF SOMEONE

FAREWELL

DRESS

TRADITIONAL DRESS

A traditional dress of Indian women is the *sari* and you will see many Indian ladies so-clad in beautiful colours and fabrics, especially Hindu ladies.

The *sari* comprises a long straight piece of fabric (six yards in length by 46 inches width) (5.5 by 1.2 metres) which is wrapped around the waist to form a long skirt. A common practice among North Indian and Muslim ladies, is to take the free end over the left shoulder and then drape it over the head. A sari is worn with a *choli* (a plain, short, fitted blouse, covering to the midriff, with elbow-length sleeves). The *sari* is normally first worn when an Indian girl turns 13 years old.

You may also see some Indian ladies wearing loose trousers, which are tight-fitting at the ankles, with a knee-length, long-sleeved, loose blouse, finished with a long scarf *(dupatta)* draped over the shoulders. This *salwar-kamez* is favoured by Sikh women, but is now commonly worn by Indian women of the younger age group.

Open sandals with heels are usual.

Indian men sometimes wear the *dhoti* (a straight piece of cloth worn around the waist, like a long sarong) with a shirt, although trousers and shirts are common, and open sandals.

TURBAN

Turbans are worn by Sikh gentlemen and can be of any colour. Saffron (sacrifice) and blue (followers of Gurus) are colours which have special significance. Sometimes a black turban is worn when in mourning, but not necessarily so. A turban, of fabric approximately five metres in length, symbolises responsibility, therefore it will depend on the individual concerned as to when he begins to wear one, although it is usually about age eight to ten years old. Prior to that, a boy will simply cover his head with a mini turban.

The dot *(pottu)* on the forehead of a Hindu woman (and some, though not all, Sikh women) may be in one of three traditional colours – red, yellow or black. Red is used by married ladies and also used simply as an auspicious colour (the basic ingredients are turmeric powder and lime juice). The yellow dot is made of sandalwood paste. Yellow is not only an auspicious colour, but it is also believed to have a calming effect and it can be put on the forehead after prayers. A black dot (sago, fried until it turns black, with added fragrance, make up this preparation) is traditionally worn by unmarried women. These days, however, almost anything is acceptable (even stick-on *pottu* of plastic or felt of various colours and shapes), so it is hard to tell what the colour signifies!

If red is worn in the centre-parting of the hair, then this does signify that the woman is married.

TRADITIONAL COLOURS

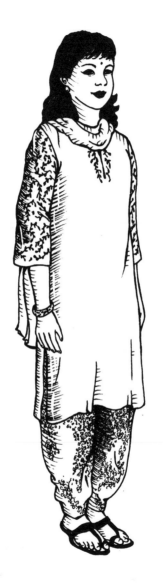

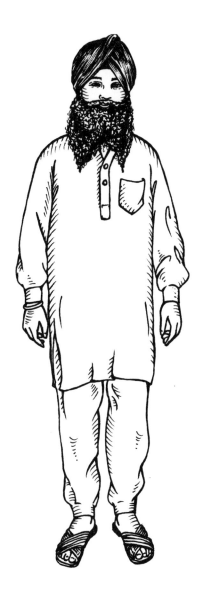

White powder *(vibooothi)*, or holy ash, can sometimes be noticed on the foreheads of both males and females, and this is usually put on during prayers, or when visiting a temple, as a reminder to Hindus that they will finally end up as ash, therefore they should constantly strive to do good deeds in this life.

Young Indian girls often wear their hair in two plaits, while married ladies wear one plait. Hair buns are often favoured by older women.

MODEST DRESSING
Do remember to dress modestly when with Indians, and choose colours other than black and white as they are traditionally for mourning. Modest dressing excludes shorts, mini-skirts, strapless and sleeveless tops.

For a casual event, ladies could wear pants and blouse.

FORMAL DRESS
For a formal Indian function such as a wedding or business dinner, if the style of dress preferred is not indicated on the invitation card, you should check with the host. To be on the safe side, upper arms should not be exposed for both ladies and gentlemen, and the same applies to knees.

A national costume is always appropriate for formal occasions.

CONVERSATION

CONVERSATION
Indians generally have a gentleness of speech and a great sense of humour. Modesty is practised when referring to themselves and

24

their families.

Questions regarding money and age are common even to mere acquaintances. If one is not used to such forthright questions, then one should not be offended, as prying is not intended.

'PRYING' QUESTIONS

Risque conversation is taboo. Do not discuss sex, politics or religion unless your host chooses to do so.

TABOO SUBJECTS

Complimenting the host's home, country and the food is always a good starter. Sports, movies and shopping also make for easy conversation.

SAFE SUBJECTS

INVITATIONS

Of course all invitations, written and verbal, must be acknowledged as soon as possible, whether accepting or declining.

INVITATIONS

Verbal invitations are often extended by Indian people, rather than written invitations. More formal functions would call for invitation cards. Colours do not play a part here.

THANK YOU

A verbal thank-you when leaving a function is normally sufficient, although a telephone call to your Indian host or hostess, the day after the function, is also welcome. Thank-you notes after special occasions are always appreciated. Flowers are not normally sent in thanks.

THANK YOU

GIFTS AND OCCASIONS

GENERAL CONSIDERATIONS

Care should be taken when selecting a gift, in order not to upset the recipient by a poor choice.

PRESENTING
A GIFT

A gift must be presented with the right hand, supported by the left hand if necessary, in the Indian way.

OPENING A GIFT

A gift is not opened in front of the giver.

COLOURS FOR
GIFT WRAPPING

Red and yellow are the colours to choose when selecting wrapping-paper, as both are considered auspicious by members of the Indian community.

TABOO GIFTS

Gifts not to give to Indians include anything connected with cows (this includes leather and related products), as the cow is considered a sacred animal because it provides milk and labour. Alcohol and cigarettes should not be given, unless you personally know that the recipient will appreciate them, and knives should also not be given as they are looked upon as weapons.

FLOWERS

Indians love flowers and look upon them as symbols of prosperity. Jasmine is the flower associated with happiness. Frangipani is used for funeral wreaths. Flower garlands, draped around the neck, are popular with Hindus and are used for celebrations and religious occasions. A garland is always presented with both hands and placed over the head onto the shoulders of the honoured person. The recipient will then place both palms together at chest level and at the same time nod gently once. This same respectful manner will be returned by the person who has presented the garland. Garlanding is normally only performed between members of the same sex.

GARLAND

Gold jewellery is always appreciated as a gift.

A gift of money is also acceptable, whatever the function, and it is presented in an envelope with the name of the giver endorsed on the back of the envelope. For an auspicious occasion, a red envelope may be used, or a white envelope with a smear of turmeric in each of the four corners. When presenting money at a funeral, a plain white envelope must be used. Money is usually given in uneven numbers, for any occasion.

A GIFT OF MONEY

AUSPICIOUS OCCASIONS

FUNERAL

A gift of money is used by the recipient to help offset the cost of the particular function. There is no 'correct' amount, though the amount is usually comparable to the cost of the individual meal provided.

AMOUNT OF CASH FOR A GIFT

The numbers one, three and nine are

NUMEROLOGY

considered auspicious, with four and eight being inauspicious.

SPECIFIC OCCASIONS AND GIFTS

HOME-COOKED MEAL

When invited by Indian friends for a home-cooked meal, sweets, fruit or chocolates are well-thought of.

NEW-BORN BABY

If you are giving a gift on the occasion of a new-born Indian baby, it is usual to give a small piece of gold jewellery to the infant, or colourful clothing.

For the Indian community, the confinement period is from one month to 44 days after birth. It is not considered good for mother and baby to venture out during this period. Although visitors are welcome at the house, it is best to check with the family concerned before visiting.

Visitors will be given a sweet, for immediate consumption, by the proud parents or grandparents, to celebrate the good news of the birth.

ENGAGEMENT

When attending an engagement party, it is not necessary to give a gift, although money is always acceptable. These days gold rings are often worn by the engaged couple, on the ring finger of the left hand.

WEDDING GIFT

At a marriage ceremony, an appropriate gift would be something for the home, preferably in cheery colours, that is both decorative and functional. Do not present ashtrays or wine glasses to Indians and do not give knives.

The gift can be presented at a Hindu wedding ceremony, to either the bride or groom, when the guests approach the couple to wish them good luck, near the end of the ceremony, after the groom has tied the marriage necklace *(thali)* on his bride. The *thali*, the equivalent of a wedding ring, is a yellow thread or chain often made of gold.

Married Indian persons wear toe rings *(mitti)* on the second toes of both feet, although the bridegroom usually only wears the rings for the marriage ceremony.

Henna (a plant dye) is used to stain palms, finger nails and toe nails of newly-married Indian persons, with the stain remaining for about three weeks.

When entering a Hindu temple, (shoes should be left neatly at the door) or an adjacent wedding hall (shoes may be kept on), guests, both males and females, will be received by members of the bride's family. Guests may then be sprinkled with rose water, given a flower and offered sandalwood mixed with rose water (a yellow paste) and *bindi* (a red paste). You dip the middle finger of your right hand in the pastes and dab your forehead or wrist, first with the sandalwood and then place the *bindi* on top of the sandalwood. The flower which is presented to a guest upon arrival at the wedding hall (given to both males and females) can be worn in the hair for women or pinned on the dress, clipped on a handbag or simply carried. Gentlemen normally place the flower nicely in their pocket, or carry it. It is considered impolite to refuse these items as they are a form of blessing for the marriage.

SEATING

If there is no usher available, guests may proceed to any seat.

Two banana trees, with flowers and fruit, at the entrance to the temple or wedding hall, are symbols of love, fertility and dedication. They also remind the bridal couple to bring up the next generation in harmony.

Hindu wedding ceremonies are quite lengthy, and midway through, a tray containing several items, including flower garlands, a coconut and the marriage necklace, is carried by a relative amongst guests. When presented to you, place both hands on the items, palms downward, and say a private blessing for the couple. Soon after, another tray, containing uncooked yellow rice, will also be carried amongst guests, who will each take a small handful. Towards the end of the wedding ceremony, when the groom ties the *thali* on his bride, guests throw the rice at the bridal couple as a blessing. At the end of the ceremony, guests proceed to the bridal couple where more yellow rice will be offered. Take some rice in each hand and sprinkle it on the bride and groom, either individually or collectively, in blessing. Start from about the shoulders of the couple and move your hands downwards, letting the rice stream out as you go along. This gesture of blessing is done three times but without replenishing the rice. This would also be the time to present your gift.

PRESENTING THE WEDDING GIFT

When a meal is served in the wedding hall after the marriage ceremony, it will be vegetarian. It is usual to eat with the fingers in typical Indian style at such an occasion — remember to use your right hand. You should observe what the Indian guests are doing, especially where they sit for eating. Different families have different customs so allow them to guide you in their ways. A sweet food is always served at Indian weddings, to ensure a sweet life ahead. It is usual to stay and chat to other guests after the meal and not rush off.

WEDDING RECEPTION

SEATING

AUSPICIOUS FARE

Guests are often presented with special sweets (*ladoo*, made with chick pea flour, sugar, cashew nuts and raisins) upon leaving a wedding reception, together with *bindi* (the red paste for marking a dot on the forehead).

When attending a Sikh wedding ceremony at a Sikh temple, or *gurdwara*, both males and females must have their heads covered. A Sikh man wears a turban and a Sikh woman dons a scarf called *dupatta*. A scarf or handkerchief is acceptable as a head covering for both sexes.

SIKH WEDDING

APPROPRIATE ATTIRE

Before entering the prayer hall in the *gurdwara*, shoes must be removed.

ARRIVAL OF GUESTS

It is usual to make a suitable mark of

respect, such as standing with head bowed for a moment, at the entrance door to the prayer hall.

PRESENTING THE
WEDDING GIFT

A guest may be received by a member of the bride's family. The wedding gift can be handed to that relative. Gifts are not presented directly to the bride or groom.

One then normally proceeds to the raised dais on which the holy book Sri Guru Granth Sahib rests and assumes a suitable respectful stance, before backing away.

SEATING

Guests will then sit facing the holy book. As seating is on the floor, ladies would be well-advised to wear pantsuits for decorum and comfort.

A Sikh marriage ceremony is short and simple. The bride and her family will humbly receive the groom and his family outside the *gurdwara*, where plain gold rings (or sometimes a gold bracelet for the bride) will be exchanged, usually worn on the ring finger of the left hand, though not necessarily so.

The couple will enter the prayer hall and sit in front of the holy book. The tying of the nuptial knot by the bride's father entails the taking of a specially embroidered saffron-coloured scarf *(pallu)*, approximately three metres long, from the groom's pocket, placing the scarf around the groom's neck and handing the other end to the bride, symbolising their joining together. The couple will then walk round the holy book four times. During the marriage ceremony prayers will be led by the priest.

Sweetmeat will be offered to the guests after the ceremony. It is impolite to refuse this item and it should be accepted using two hands.

Upon leaving the prayer hall, it is usual to stand for a moment with head bowed as a mark of respect.

After the marriage ceremony, which must be performed before noon, guests will partake of lunch.

It is customary for friends of the bride to enjoy a vegetarian meal in the dining hall of the *gurdwara*. You will need to be guided by other guests as to the wearing, or not, of shoes, as the practice varies from *gurdwara* to *gurdwara*. The style of eating (cutlery or fingers) will depend on the setting.

Tables will be laid out in straight lines and seating arrangements will be at the host's discretion. Males and females may be seated separately. Again, you should observe what the Sikh guests are doing, as different families have different customs.

Upon leaving, guests will be presented with sweets (*ladoo,* or *jalabee* — deep-fried rose-flavoured coils of batter) or fruit (apples are popular) by the bride's representatives.

Meanwhile, the bridal party and friends of the groom will be entertained at a reception, in a restaurant or at home, by the bride's parents. The choice of food would have been previously decided on by the hosts, with beef being excluded as it is not considered socially acceptable. Seating arrangements will be at the host's discretion and the style of eating will depend on the setting. Parting gifts to guest are not usual.

BIRTHDAY

For a birthday party, the same etiquette applies pertaining to gifts, dress and eating as for other happy occasions within the Indian community. A sweet food is always served, symbolising a sweet life.

HOUSEWARMING

A housewarming ceremony is often held when an Indian family moves to their new home. A Hindu priest will attend and offer prayers for the cleansing and purification of

HINDU HOUSEHOLD

a Hindu household. He will also sprinkle holy water throughout the house and on all persons present. A suitable housewarming gift would be a household item. Vegetarian food will be served and also a sweet dish, to ensure sweetness in the new home.

At special occasions it is usual to serve *payasam* which is a milk-based sweet porridge made with rice or vermicelli and nuts, sugar and fruit.

SIKH HOUSEHOLD

A Sikh priest will attend a housewarming, ceremoniously bearing the holy book, to offer prayers and read holy words in a Sikh household. Furniture will normally be stored away in order that guests can sit on the floor. Vegetarian food will be served. A household item would be a suitable gift, and should be presented to the host. All present will have their heads covered, as the house is considered a temple for the day, due to the presence of the holy book borne by the priest.

FUNERAL

FLORAL / MONETARY CONTRIBUTION

If confronted with the necessity to attend the funeral of an Indian person, a floral wreath may be sent. If you prefer, money may be given to the family, presented in a white envelope with the giver's name endorsed on the back of the envelope. However, as different families practise different customs, it would be best to seek advice from others assembled at such a gathering.

APPROPRIATE ATTIRE

When visiting the home to pay your respects, sombre colours should be worn.

After approaching the family of the deceased, it is customary to view the body and stand with head bowed for a few moments.

Unless unavoidable, Hindus and Sikhs must be cremated within 24 hours after death. Muslims are buried within 12 hours of death. Christian and Buddhist burials or cremations take place within a few days of death occurring.

Some Indians prefer the men-folk only to attend the funeral, so females should inquire from the bereaved family of their wishes.

After the body has left the house, refreshments may be served to visitors who remain at the home.

TAKING LEAVE

It is best not to say goodbye to the bereaved family, but rather to leave quietly.

TEMPLE AND GURDWARA

Any persons who enter a Hindu temple or Sikh *gurdwara*, for any reason, must first

Dining Etiquette

PRE-MEAL
Relaxed conversation, in the living room, usually precedes a home-cooked meal.

The serving, or not, of pre-meal drinks and snacks will depend on the custom of your Indian host. You may be asked if you would like alcohol, but remember that not all Indians consume alcohol due to religious beliefs. Fruit juice or a soft drink would be a more prudent choice.

If snacks are offered, they might include *vadai* (deep-fried cakes made with ground lentils, green chillies and ginger), *muruku* (pretzel-like, crispy and crunchy), *pakhora* (mixed vegetable fritters) and *samosa* (deep-fried pastry containing meat, onion and spices).

SEATING AT THE TABLE
Depending on how traditional your hosts are, you may find yourself seated Western-style, or seated on a floor mat at a low rectangular table. Also, the sexes may be segregated, with the men eating first, being

served by the women. However, if the meal is taken together as a family then the head of the family will normally sit at the head of the table, with his wife at the other end.

As an honoured guest, you may find yourself at the head of the table, with the head of the family seated to the side. It is usual for the guest-of-honour to be seated to the host's right.

Females group together and males sit together at the table in such a family setting.

As a guest, you will be invited by your Indian host to be seated first.

If you are eating in a fine Indian restaurant, the host (or hostess) will take the place at the head of the table and females will group together and males will sit together. If there is a guest-of-honour, he or she will sit next to the host.

TABLE SETTINGS

WITH THALI

In a traditional Indian home, the table may be set with *thali*. A *thali* is a metal tray with several small matching metal bowls for food, or a metal tray with indentations to hold food. All the food, including dessert, is served at the same time, with the rice or bread placed in the centre of the individual tray.

WITH BANANA LEAF

Then again, South Indian food might be served on a large banana leaf which has a tipped end or is rectangular, placed with the glossy side facing upwards, the stem parallel

to the diner. Leaves are disposed of after use. Eating from a banana leaf is thought to bring wealth, health and happiness.

In both instances, cutlery is not used for eating, unless requested, as Indians generally eat with fingers.

The setting could also be more Western in style, with individual plates, forks and spoons. The fork will be placed to the left and the spoon to the right of the individual plate. Knives are not used. A spoon is used to cut large portions of food. Serving bowls

WITH CUTLERY

of food will be placed in the centre of the table, with serving spoons.

A tumbler for water is placed to the left of each style of setting.

Any of the above settings may be seen in Indian restaurants, depending on where you choose to eat.

BREAKFAST, LUNCH AND DINNER

Dhal (lentils) are served with most Indian meals, including breakfast.

Breakfast favourites are *idli* (ground lentils and rice mixture, fermented and steamed in moulds), *thosai* (Indian-style pancake) and *vadai* (deep fried cakes made with ground lentils, green chillies and ginger). They are all served with coconut chutney. *Roti paratha* (rich, flaky bread served with curry sauce) is also popular.

Breakfast, Indian style, is almost always accompanied by tea or coffee, with fresh milk and sugar usually added before serving. *Lassi* (a yoghurt drink served sweet, natural or salted) is also a good beverage to start the day.

An Indian lunch often consists of *chapati* (round, unleavened, wholemeal bread) served with a curry of meat, fish or vegetables. Fish Head Curry is a firm favourite, also *murtabak* (flaky Indian bread filled with spicy minced meat and onions).

Fresh fruit is often served as a dessert.

Water is the usual drink with lunch.

If you choose a set lunch, or dinner, in an Indian restaurant the setting is likely to be *thali* and you can be sure of a representative Indian meal.

All the dishes of food at an Indian meal are generally served together. The dishes are all shared amongst your party in some restaurants, while in others individual dishes or *thalis* are served.

Indian bread is placed at one's left-hand side, or in the centre of the *thali*. It does not require butter as a spread.

Rice, if eaten, will be served in the centre of the plate or banana leaf and the various curries and accompaniments will be placed on the plate or leaf around the rice, in small portions — similar to a *thali* setting.

Indian desserts are sweet and rich and fruit is also often offered. Dried fruit, especially raisins, is popular.

At a South Indian vegetarian restaurant, I was happily eating *thali* style and did not realise that the dessert was in one of the many bowls on my tray and I blithely ate the dessert as part of the main meal!

Do check if you are unsure of anything. Your Indian host or the service staff will normally be most happy to enlighten you about their food.

TEA
Indians, in general, love drinking tea and often invite friends to join them at home for

this pleasure.

TEA AND COFFEE

Hot favourites are tea for North Indians and coffee for South Indians, with fresh milk and sugar usually added before serving. Cardamoms are often used instead of sugar to flavour tea, this drink being called *masala* tea.

Popular cold drinks include fresh lime juice and *lassi*.

SNACKS

With morning and afternoon tea, nuts are often offered. Cashewnuts are popular with South Indians and pistachios with North Indians. A variety of milk-based sweets is also enjoyed, as are savoury *samosa* and *pakhora*.

Any-time Indian snacks include *idli* and *thosai*. Both are made from a mixture of ground lentils and rice. Coconut chutney accompanies both.

EATING AND DRINKING

Food is eaten in the Indian manner with the right hand and the left hand is used for drinks, although if no food is consumed then the right hand is used for drinks.

PLACING YOUR ORDER

STAPLE FOOD

Rice *(chawal)* is always on the menu and is a staple food, as is bread *(roti)*.

DIFFERENT STYLES

Indian food, broadly speaking, is vegetarian and non-vegetarian, also North Indian and South Indian.

South Indian food features rice and really hot dishes, whereas North Indian food has wheat flour (bread) and mild, spicy dishes.

Sambar (lentil and vegetable puree) is a popular South Indian dish as are lentils *(dhal),* also favourites in North Indian cuisine. *Paneer* (cottage cheese) is often added to North Indian dishes, and plain yoghurt and buttermilk are often served with South Indian dishes. With both North and South Indian food, *papadam* or *uppalum* (crispy lentil-based crackers), are usually served.

It is usual, when ordering *a la carte,* to choose a fish dish, one meat or chicken dish, a lentil dish, one or two vegetable dishes and chutney, and bread if you wish..

Ideally, a balance of tastes, textures, colours and aromas should be considered when ordering.

Remember that the dishes are shared amongst the diners. If food is served in central serving dishes, each person helps himself, or herself, from the various central dishes as and when wished throughout the meal.

If food is served by a waiter onto individual banana leaves, you may ask for more, if desired.

A variety of sweet desserts is common in Indian cuisine. For examples, see the section on Food, Glorious Food!

If you are eating alone, there are set meals and many Indian one-dish meals to choose from. Chicken Briyani (saffron rice cooked with chicken), Vegetable Briyani (saffron rice cooked with vegetables), fish curry, *murtabak* (flaky Indian bread filled with spicy minced meat and onions), *thosai* (Indian-style pancake), *puri* (deep fried wholemeal bread, usually served with potato *masala*) and *Mee Goreng* (fried noodles) are popular one-dish meals.

If you have Indian Muslim guests, *halal* (acceptable) food is served at some Indian establishments, therefore check beforehand with the eating place of your choice. *Halal* food is that which has been processed, cooked or prepared according to Islamic law. For instance, meat and poultry must be slaughtered by a Muslim to be *halal*. Any part of a pig and any product derived from that animal are *haram* (forbidden). Liquor and any intoxicating substances are also forbidden. Ducks, frogs and turtles are also not favoured by Muslims.

It should be noted that the cow is held in respect for its service to mankind, and many Indians, including Hindus and Buddhists, do not eat beef. Sikhs also do not eat beef. Many Buddhists also do not eat eggs, and many Indians are strict vegetarians.

Meatless days also feature in the dietary habits of many Indians, depending on the particular deity worshipped.

When you are entertaining Indian guests, whether at home or out, be sure and check beforehand that your choice of food is acceptable, simply by asking your guests. Similarly, as a guest, you should inform your host beforehand of any dietary restrictions that you may have. As an act of courtesy to your guests, or hosts, and to make them feel more comfortable, you could refrain from eating prohibited food in their company. You may also wish to forego alcohol.

INDIAN VEGETARIAN FOOD

If you are ordering an Indian vegetarian meal, you may wish to include a lentil dish as lentils are popular and are the main source of protein for vegetarians.

Rice is the staple food for most South Indians.

Vadai is a popular starter – deep-fried cake made with ground lentils, green chillies and ginger.

It is usual to order three vegetable dishes (including lentils) and two curry items, choosing different textures, tastes and colours. The choice is great – peas, ladies fingers, potatoes, cauliflower, corn, nuts, *paneer* (cottage cheese), vermicelli – and the choice is yours. *Raita* (salad mixed with yoghurt) is also popular. Or you may order a potato dish, a curry dish and *raita*.

Some Indian vegetarians do not include onions and garlic in their cooking as they do not like to kill the whole plant when picking the vegetables.

Remember that the dishes are all shared amongst your party in some restaurants, while in others individual dishes/*thali* are

45

served.

Indian vegetarian desserts include those made with semolina, vermicelli, rice, nuts or sago, and fresh fruit is usually available.

ORDERING
FOOD

In an Indian restaurant, a male guest places the order with the waiter, and a female guest gives her order to the host. If your party is large, you should decide amongst yourselves which dishes to order, and one person should place the order with the waiter.

If you do not have an Indian friend to assist you with any of the meals, then ask the waiter for advice on ordering.

For gastronomic delights, see the section on Food, Glorious Food!

ORDERING
DRINKS

TEA AND
COFFEE

Tea or coffee, with fresh milk and sugar added before serving, often ends a meal. *Masala* tea (tea with fresh milk, flavoured with cardamoms instead of sugar) is popular.

COLD DRINKS

Lassi (a yoghurt drink) complements an Indian meal, as does *Bhadum Kheer* (an almond-based milk drink).

Beer may be ordered in a licensed restaurant, if desired, but remember that not all Indians consume alcohol due to religious beliefs.

Table Etiquette

Men are seated before women and are also served first.

A silent prayer may be offered by the host before a meal. One should simply bow one's head as a mark of respect.

PRAYER

It is usual for the Indian host to say, *"Sapudungal"* (please eat) before eating, to which guests can simply reply with, "thank you".

INVITATION TO BEGIN EATING

The host will begin the meal by handing a serving bowl to the guest of honour to serve himself. The host will serve himself last. As a guest, you should always wait to be offered food, initially.

GUEST OF HONOUR TO BEGIN

In the traditional Indian style of eating, food is eaten with the fingers. Hands are therefore always washed before and after meals, whether eating at home or out. Wash-basins may be visible at restaurants.

It is usual to be offered a finger bowl and small towel for the washing and drying of your fingers. Upon completion, the used section of the towel is folded inwards and

FINGER BOWL

the towel is placed neatly next to the finger bowl. Alternatively, you may be directed to a hand-basin.

Eating with the fingers is easier said than done! Only the right hand is used for eating purposes. Being left-handed I find it even more difficult!

I know of an Indian gentleman, left-handed from birth, whose mother despaired of ever teaching him good manners. 23 years on, he met and courted a young Indian lady and, within a matter of weeks, was eating perfectly with his right hand! "Marry her!", exclaimed his delighted mother, without any other knowledge of the girl. Good manners maketh a good marriage!

To eat with the fingers, just take a small amount of food and mound it smoothly, then, fingertips facing upwards, put the food quickly into your mouth, using your thumb to push the food in. Try not to spill any food and not to lick your fingers in the process. Take care not to get your palms involved, only your fingertips should be used.

If it proves really difficult, then request a fork and spoon. Food is eaten from the spoon, not from the fork, using the right hand. The fork is used with the concave side of the tines to the diner, to push the food onto the spoon.

You may use your left hand for the passing of dishes and utensils if your right hand is sticky from eating. The lightly clenched fist of your right hand, palm downwards, should support your left arm, to show respect in using your right hand.

If you are eating with a fork and spoon, then use your right hand to pass the serving dishes.

Drinking glasses are also held in the left hand when the right hand is sticky.

Do not serve food to another person using your own utensils.

When serving yourself from a central serving bowl, use the serving spoon. The common serving spoons must never touch the food on the individual plates, so do take care. The food must be placed on the far (top) side of your plate or leaf each time.

Sour food is placed on the left and less sour dishes are served in a clockwise direction, at the top of your receptacle.

Various condiments are served in small containers with small serving spoons. They include toasted coconut, a variety of chutneys, dried fish, diced tomatoes and cucumber, and lentil wafers. You help yourself to all or any of the condiments prior to eating your meal, by placing them neatly on your plate or leaf. Or, you indicate to the waiter and he will serve you. The condiments may be tasted as you wish throughout the meal. More may be requested as the meal progresses, if desired. Also, extra curry sauce can be requested.

FOOD WRAPPED IN LEAVES

Any food served wrapped in leaves should be opened up properly before beginning eating the meal, otherwise your fingers will become too sticky as the meal progresses to do the job properly.

BANANA LEAF SERVICE

In a traditional South Indian setting, a banana leaf may be used in place of a plate. Serving of food follows a set pattern. First, *payasam* or a sweet dish is served on the bottom right corner of the leaf. Then a variety of side dishes, starting from the top right corner of the leaf. Depending on the occasion, the number of dishes will range from three to nine. Banana chips, *papadam* and pickles are next. The staple food, rice, is then served. *Dhal* (lentils) and *ghee* (clarified butter) are served next, to be mixed with the rice using fingers.

The first course, *sambar* (lentil-based curry) will then be served onto the rice. After eating the first course, the second course, *rasam* (a light peppery soup), will be served. This is eaten mixed with a fresh portion of rice – the section on SOUP will be useful here. Then the final course of plain yoghurt and/

50

or buttermilk will be served, to be mixed with a fresh portion of rice before eating.

The condiments are consumed as and when wished throughout the meal. They will be replenished often.

If you are unable to finish eating all the rice for each course, simply push it neatly with your fingers a little to the left side in order to make space for the fresh serving of rice.

Sometimes the *payasam* or sweet will be served as a separate course after the second course. It is customarily eaten after the final course of yoghurt.

This order of serving and eating is designed as an aid to digestion.

The meal commences only after all the side dishes and rice, *dhal* and *ghee* have been served onto the banana leaf, or when the host invites guests to eat.

Eating is done quietly, chewing with the mouth closed.

It is customary to begin an Indian meal by eating one or two mouthfuls of rice first, rice being the principal food. Begin with the rice nearest to you on your plate, *thali* or leaf.

If only one type of food is tasted in one mouthful, then you can savour the taste of each dish. On the other hand, if you mix small portions of several types of food and rice together for one mouthful then you experience a whole myriad of tastes. Always mix other food with rice, not the other way round. The blandness of the rice offsets the spiciness of the other dishes.

Rice stays in the centre of your leaf, *thali* or plate and is not moved around.

Cucumber and yoghurt are often available as side dishes, and these are real coolers for a burning mouth! To finish your main course with these is usual.

To eat bread, use both hands to tear the bread, tearing a small piece at the time you want to eat it. It is acceptable to scoop up curry and other food from your plate with the bread as you proceed through the meal, again using your right hand.

Some Indian desserts and sweets are decorated with edible silver leaf. I wonder how many unknowing diners have discarded the expensive ingredient, thinking it to be inedible!

A HOME-COOKED MEAL

When eating a home-cooked Indian meal, serve yourself small portions from three or four dishes to begin, then have second helpings later. To ask for seconds is to compliment the hostess.

FINISHING A MEAL

It is good etiquette at an Indian meal to finish eating all the rice on one's plate or leaf. All persons at the table should endeavour to finish the meal at the same time.

When eating *thali* style, the bowls are left neatly on the tray after the meal is finished.

When using a banana leaf for your South Indian meal, the leaf should be folded upwards in half towards the centre of the table after the meal. If a fork and spoon are used with a banana leaf, they should be placed side by side on top of the folded banana leaf upon finishing.

For an Indian meal with a Western setting, the fork and spoon are placed side by side on the individual dinner plate after eating a meal, with the handles towards the diner.

FINGERS

Do not let food dry on your fingers as it is considered impolite. It is quite in order to go to the wash-basin, whether in a home or restaurant, after a meal. In a restaurant where table napkins are provided, fingers may be wiped gently on the napkins, and a wash-basin used.

DIGESTIVE

After an Indian meal *paan* may be served. This consists of betel fruit and leaves (from the areca palm and the pan plant) with a spice mixture. It is believed that *paan* acts as a digestive and cleanses the mouth. Go slowly though, as it is really spicy! *Paan* can either be eaten, or chewed and then spat into a spittoon. Sometimes a small container with spices (caraway seeds, cloves, aniseed) and rock sugar will be offered in place of the more traditional *paan*. These are for eating as an aid to digestion and to give a pleasant aroma to the breath.

It is customary after a meal to say, "*Nandrī*" (thank you) to your Tamil Indian host, and the host will respond with, "Was everything to your satisfaction?" "Thank you" in English is also proper.

The host will normally leave the table first.

TAKING LEAVE AFTER A MEAL

It is not customary to take one's leave immediately after a meal in an Indian home, but rather to stay a short time engaging in conversation before departing.

A reciprocal meal is always appreciated by Indian hosts, bearing in mind dietary factors.

SPECIFIC INDIAN FOOD

FISH HEAD CURRY

Fish Head Curry is one favourite Indian dish which may be difficult to eat for first timers. Cooked with coconut milk, tamarind, curry leaves, onions, tomatoes, ladies fingers and spices, the fish head and fragrant curry sauce are served in a central serving bowl, with a serving ladle. Snapper is popular, as the head has succulent flesh and only a few small bones.

You help yourself to the fish, using the ladle, and place some flesh and vegetables at the top of your plate or leaf. The curry sauce is gently ladled onto your rice. Be sure that the serving ladle does not touch the food on your individual plate or leaf.

The beauty of eating with the fingers is evident with this particular dish, as it is extremely easy to separate any bones from the fish before actually eating.

From the portion of fish served on to your plate or leaf, use the fingers of your right hand and pick the flesh from the bones. Discarded bones must be placed together neatly at the top of your plate or leaf, although sometimes a small plate especially for the bones is provided.

Using your right hand, mix the fish with some rice and enjoy your meal.

Be sure and wash your hands well, using soap, after eating, as some spices tend to stain the fingers if not properly washed off.

SOUP

At an Indian meal, soup is served in one central soup tureen, with a soup ladle. SOUP

Soup is consumed as part of the meal, not prior to it and not all at one time.

It is primarily for moistening the rice and MOISTENING THE RICE not only for drinking on its own. You simply take some soup stock from the tureen, using the soup ladle, and pour it gently on the rice on your own plate or leaf.

Solid soup ingredients are removed from the central tureen, using the soup ladle, and placed neatly on your own plate or leaf, to the far (top) side.

If by chance you are served with a small individual bowl of soup, the same etiquette applies as for the central soup tureen, although you can use your spoon to consume the soup if you prefer. The left hand may be used for this purpose if your right hand is sticky from eating.

If you are using a soup spoon, the spoon remains in the soup bowl upon finishing, the handle towards the diner.

BONES

BONES AND
INEDIBLE
MATTER
All bones and other inedible matter must be placed neatly on the top (far) side of your plate or leaf.

No bones or food are placed on the table when eating Indian style.

EATING MEAT
FROM A BONE
When eating meat from a bone, the fingers of the right hand must be used to pick the meat off the bone. The bone must remain on the plate.

At the end of an Indian meal, any leftovers on your plate or leaf should be pushed neatly to the centre of your receptacle.

SERVIETTES/TABLE NAPKINS

When eating Indian style, serviettes or table

napkins, as such, are not always available.

A table napkin, if provided, should be kept on the diner's lap except when being used to gently wipe the mouth or hands. The soiled section should be folded inwards at the conclusion of the meal and the folded serviette placed neatly on the table next to your setting.

In a home setting there will often be a finger-bowl on the table for use before and after eating. Diners should wash and dry their fingers gently, then fold the used section of the towel inwards before placing the towel next to the finger-bowl neatly.

You may ask to use a hand-basin, whether at home or eating out, if your fingers are oily.

I always find it helpful to carry a handkerchief or tissues with me in case of need — wet eyes and nose from the curry!

BUFFET

Indian meals are not traditionally served buffet style. When an Indian meal is presented in such a style, it is approached in the same manner as for a Western buffet meal – you help yourself to food from a long table laden with food and return to your own table to eat. You may return to the buffet table for more helpings of food throughout the meal. In other words, take numerous small helpings, not a large quantity piled high.

It is important to always keep the food in

the serving receptacles looking neat by helping yourself carefully and taking the food nearest to you from the containers.

BUSINESS

Indian business men and women are astute and combine business logic and manners with good humour.

The same 'rules' apply to invitations, dress and the giving and receiving of business cards, as with most other Asian societies, meaning that replies are expected, modest attire, and the using of both hands for the giving and receiving of business cards.

Festive Fare

Hindus celebrate the joyous Deepavali festival on the new moon of the seventh month of the Hindu calendar (October or November) annually.

The seventh lunar month of the Hindu calendar is called *Aippasi* in Tamil.

For this 'Festival of Lights', marking the triumph of good over evil and light over darkness, homes are at their best. Rows of small earthern-ware oil lamps are lit to welcome Lakshmi, the Goddess of Wealth, who is believed to visit clean and neat Hindu homes at Deepavali.

Homes will look festive with fresh mango leaves strung at the entrance, each leaf having a dot of sandalwood paste, and a dab of *bindi* on top of the sandalwood dot. There must be an odd number of leaves for this decoration. A large lamp with wicks may also be seen, and a tray containing rosewater, *bindi* and fresh flowers.

A week before Deepavali, prayers are said at home for departed relatives, and special food offerings made by family members.

Hindu businessmen consider Deepavali an auspicious time to open new account books as a sign of bright new beginnings.

CLOTHING

At dawn on Deepavali Day, when light takes over from darkness, Hindus greet the new beginning dressed in colourful new clothes. Beautiful *saris* and gold jewellery will be worn by ladies, with fresh flowers adorning their hair.

After praying at home and at the temple, family ties will be re-affirmed by visiting relatives. Friends are always welcome on this festive day.

FESTIVE FARE

Hindus traditionally serve vegetarian food for Deepavali.

A typical vegetarian meal will include a variety of vegetables (prepared in different styles of cooking and using a variety of spices), rice or bread, soup and dessert. *Payasam* (a milk-based sweet porridge made with rice or vermicelli and nuts, sugar and fruit) is a festive dessert that will be seen on many tables.

At home, a variety of sweets and savouries will be served to relatives and friends who visit. *Muruku*, a pretzel-like crispy and crunchy snack, is a favourite. Festive sweets include *ladoo* (made with chick pea flour, sugar, cashew nuts and raisins) and *rasagolla* (cottage cheese fried in ghee and mixed with sugar syrup).

Drinks include *Bhadum Kheer* (an almond-based milk drink), fresh milk, tea, coffee and soft drinks.

As a guest, one should eat and drink the host's offerings at such an important festival. To refuse is impolite.

Sweets are customarily presented as gifts to relatives and friends, signifying the giving of sweetness to each other. Many of the sweets are milk-based and contain nuts.

FESTIVE GIFT

Envelopes containing money in odd numbers are given to children as good luck gifts by relatives and friends during the Deepavali celebrations. The envelopes used will either be white with a smear of turmeric in each of the four corners, or any colourful envelope. As a general guide and depending on one's familiarity with the family, between $5 and $21 would be an appropriate amount.

MONETARY GIFT

The usual greeting is, *"Deepavali Valthugal"* (Deepavali greetings).

SPOKEN GREETING

Food, Glorious Food!

STAPLE FOOD **Rice *(chawal)* is a principal item in an Indian meal, as is bread *(roti)*.**

Indian cuisine is not all hot curries. It also features coconut, chilli, yoghurt and spices. *Dhal* (lentils) are served at most meals, valued for their protein content. Cereals also play an important role, as do milk products.

NORTH INDIAN Mildly spiced food is predominant in North Indian cuisine, and from Kashmir and Punjab come dishes such as *tandoor* (clay oven) cooking. Tandoori Chicken and Tandoori Fish are justly famous. Also, *korma* (rich, thick, pale-coloured curry with meat, poultry or fish), *briyani* (saffron rice cooked with chicken or mutton or vegetables) and kebabs (minced meat with spices, threaded on skewers and barbecued). Wheat flour is an important item in North Indian cooking, more so than rice.

SIKH The Sikhs' staple diet includes *dhal* (lentils) and *chapati* (bread). Keema Mattar (minced meat with peas) is a popular dish, usually eaten with *chapati*.

Briyani (saffron rice with chicken, mutton or vegetables) is a favourite food of Indian Muslims.

INDIAN MUSLIM

Really hot dishes are featured in South Indian cuisine. *Vindaloo* (meat or poultry marinated with vinegar and spices, cooked in a tangy piquant sauce), Madras curries, and Prawn Curry are just some of the favourites.

SOUTH INDIAN

Sambar (lentil and vegetable puree), eaten with rice or *idli* (rice cake) is a well-known vegetarian dish.

VEGETARIAN

Popular breads include *chapati* (thin, flat, unleavened wholemeal bread, cooked on a griddle, from North India), *naan* (leavened white bread, cooked in a *tandoor* oven, from Punjab), *puri* (deep-fried wholemeal bread, eaten with curry gravy, popular with South Indians) and *roti paratha* (flaky wholemeal bread, cooked on a griddle, an Indian Muslim favourite).

BREAD

Other Indian favourites, apart from rice, bread, vegetables lentils and chutney in many styles, include *Roganjosh* (mutton and spices in yoghurt), Fish Head Curry, mulligatawny (literally, chilli water) soup and *rasam* (a pepper water soup, popular as an aid to digestion).

OTHER FAVOURITES

For dessert, *payasam* (a milk-based, sweet, thick, porridge made with rice or vermicelli and nuts, sugar and fruit) from South India is a favourite. *Kulfi* (Indian-style ice cream garnished with pistachio nuts),

DESSERT

originating in North India, is a real cooler. Or try *Gelab Jamun* (a milk-based dessert in syrup). *Ras Malai* (cream cheese balls in milk) is also a rich and popular dessert. A Sikh favourite is *kheer*, a boiled, sweet, milk-based rice pudding containing almonds, with brown sugar sprinkled on top. *Halwa* is a popular Indian Muslim dessert. Eaten with the fingers, the orange-coloured sweet is made of rice flour, brown sugar, ghee and nuts. Or ask for desserts made with semolina, vermicelli, nuts or sago. Be forewarned, Indian desserts are – no, not hot – extremely sweet and rich.

"Sapudungal"
Please eat!

Malay Etiquette

The Malay people have a strong sense of community spirit and they place great emphasis on *Adab* or mannerism – being helpful, polite, considerate and courteous – as this reflects on their own characters.

MALAY COMMUNITY

Malays live in happy, close-knit family circles, where courtesy and respect are a way of life. They are known for their gentle mannerisms.

The Islamic religion, founded in the seventh century A.D., is an integral part of everyday Malay life. Muslims, adherents to Islam, believe in one God, Allah, and they pray five times a day facing Mecca, Saudi Arabia, the birthplace of the faith.

ISLAM

The Muslim calendar is based on the moon.

CALENDAR

GREETINGS
The traditional Malay gesture, upon meeting and taking leave, is for both parties to proffer two hands each and very gently touch each other's hands (similar to a brief

TRADITIONAL GREETING

handshake), then lightly touch their own hearts with the fingers of both hands. This is known as *salam* and is only performed between members of the same sex.

HANDSHAKE

These days, shaking hands Western style is often done between men, especially with foreigners. Muslim ladies do not shake hands with, or touch, males. Be guided by the actions of the Malay lady upon being introduced. A smile and a gentle nod of the head may be the appropriate gesture.

OPENING REMARK

"Where are you going?" is a common opening remark by Malay persons, not really a question, and the reply may be a simple, "For a walk".

NAMES

SURNAME

Malays do not have surnames. They often introduce themselves by using their first name, say, Ali, or by adding their father's name as in Ali Sulaiman, or Ali *bin* Sulaiman (*bin* is equivalent to 'son of'). In all cases, you should refer to him as *Encik* Ali —

PERSONAL NAME

'*Encik*' (pronounced En-chek) denotes 'Mister' — or, if you prefer, Mr Ali. When greeting a Malay lady, also use her own name, say, Salmah, but add *Cik* (pronounced Chek) in front, as in *Cik* Salmah, or Miss Salmah. She may be Salmah Ali or Salmah *binti* (daughter of) Ali. If you know that she is a married lady you may address her as *Puan* Salmah. A married Malay woman does not necessarily take her husband's name upon marriage, but often retains her father's name. As can be seen, names only carry on for one generation.

FEMALE NAME

MARRIED NAME

A Muslim gentleman is entitled to add the prefix '*Haji*' to his name – as in *Haji* Ali – when he has made a holy pilgrimage *(Haj)* to Mecca in fulfilment of part of his religious obligations. Likewise, a Muslim lady will add '*Hajjah*' as, for example, *Hajjah* Salmah.

HAJI AND HAJJAH

Malaysian titles (awards of the Order of Chivalry) one may come across include *Tun*, *Tan Sri* and *Datuk*. Names will be prefixed by such titles, as in *Datuk* Ali *bin* Sulaiman. The wife of a *Datuk* is addressed as *Datin*, the wife of a *Tun* is known as *Toh Puan* and the wife of a *Tan Sri* is called *Puan Sri*.

TITLES

INTRODUCTIONS
When performing introductions in the Malay manner, the older or most respected person's name is mentioned first. A woman's name is mentioned before a gentleman's name when introducing the two.

ORDER OF INTRODUCTIONS

It is polite to address older persons as 'Aunty' *(Ma Cik)* or 'Uncle' *(Pa Cik)* even though you are not a relative.

VISITING A MALAY HOME

Most Malays enjoy extending their traditional hospitality and inviting friends to their homes.

There are many *pantang larang* (dos and don'ts) in the Malay culture and it is good if one has at least an understanding of some of them.

When visiting a Malay home, it is often the host who greets the guests upon their arrival, with the hostess remaining indoors.

It is customary to remove your shoes before entering a Malay home and leave them neatly at the entrance. The entrance might be a door or a small flight of steps leading up to a verandah in a traditional Malay-style house. If the latter, then your shoes should be left at the bottom step. This is done not only for hygienic purposes, but also to keep the house clean for prayers.

A Muslim home has a prayer rug on the floor and care should be taken by a guest not to stand or sit on the prayer rug. Also, a guest must not touch the Koran, the Islamic holy book, without first asking permission. If in doubt, it is far better to ask a question of your Malay host than to unwittingly commit a gaffe.

Muslims have five set times each day for

prayer, at dawn, noon, afternoon, dusk and evening. The times are approximately 5.30 a.m., 1 p.m., 5 p.m., 7 p.m. and 8.30 p.m., with each prayer approximately five minutes in duration. If you are visiting a Malay home unannounced, avoid prayer times, allowing time also for preparation (ablutions) for prayers.

Followers of Islam are not permitted to touch dogs. If a Muslim person visits you and you own a dog, it would be best to keep your dog out of sight.

DOGS

Do not sit until your Malay host invites you to do so. The host will say, *"Jemput duduk"* or, *"Sila duduk"* which means, "Please sit down."

SEATING

In a traditional Malay home, you may find yourself seated on a mat on the floor. Do not sit directly in front of the door. Men often sit cross-legged, while women never do this, but place their legs together to either side, with feet tucked away. However, when seated on a chair, it is best not to cross one leg over the other and not to expose the soles of one's feet as this is considered most impolite.

If the wife of the host does not join you it is simply that this is part of her upbringing. Often, the men congregate together and the women elsewhere in the house.

Even if you call unexpectedly on a Malay family, you will almost certainly be served with a drink and snack, in a most gracious

WHEN OFFERED A DRINK

71

manner. After being invited to, do eat and drink at least a little, as it is impolite not to do so. To be urged several times to begin shows your politeness in not being greedy. It is good manners to leave a little, whether food or drink.

Likewise, you should always offer your Malay guest a light refreshment and it should be presented on a tray.

GREETING ELDERS

When an older person enters the room, it is usual to rise. Always remember to greet older people ('Aunty' or 'Uncle'), even without an introduction.

SMOKING

To refrain from smoking would be extremely wise, as would whistling indoors. To blow one's nose in company is also a breach of etiquette in the Malay way.

USE OF LEFT HAND

Do not use your left hand for any occasion, as it is considered impolite to do so in Malay society. The left hand is used for toilet purposes.

When giving or receiving an item, the right hand must be used, supported by the left hand if necessary.

BODY-TOUCHING

Refrain from body-touching between opposite sexes as this is not considered proper by the Malay community and is indeed a grave matter. Even casual touching is taboo. Caucasians, in particular, are a 'touching' people and should be aware of this.

POINTING

If you wish to point in the presence of Malays use your right thumb only, fold your fingers to your palm and keep your palm sideways. To use your index finger to point is considered insulting. It is also impolite to point or indicate by using your shoe or foot.

To beckon, you wave your right hand, fingers outstretched downwards but together and the palm facing towards your body.

BECKONING

When passing in front of a Malay person, or persons, it is polite to extend your right arm, fingers outstretched but together, showing the direction in which you are walking, at say, a 30 degree angle, with the left arm falling naturally. Bow slightly whilst walking and say, "Excuse me".

WHEN PASSING IN FRONT OF SOMEONE

Remember that Malays are gentle people, and it is wise to practise decorum in all ways.

When taking leave of a Malay family, it is not usual to say goodbye but rather utter a phrase asking permission to leave, such as, "I'll be leaving now, if you don't mind."

FAREWELL

DRESS

Muslims have a strict dress code. Muslim women, traditionally, dress modestly and may cover the entire body with only face, hands and feet exposed.

Heads are covered by Muslim females as a sign of humility or modesty. Dressed in their *baju kurong* (long-sleeved, high rounded neck-line, three-quarter length loose blouse, worn over an ankle-length sarong or skirt), Malay women look most attractive.

Leather, and sequin, sandals or open-toe shoes are popular, with high or low heels. For formal wear, matching sandals and bag are usual.

Malay men may wear long-sleeved shirts (also called *baju kurong*) over long sarongs, although trousers and shirts are common nowadays. Leather sandals are usual.

When a Muslim gentleman wears a white skull-cap it indicates that he has made a holy pilgrimage *(Haj)* to Mecca. Similarly, a Muslim lady who has performed a pilgrimage usually wears a white scarf on special occasions. Nowadays, colourful scarfs are popular, though white is preferable signifying purity, with sins blotted out.

Do, of course, remember to dress modestly when with Malays, and choose colours that are not sombre or all-white as they are traditionally for mourning. Dressing modestly means no shorts, mini-skirts, strapless and sleeveless tops. It is preferable to cover the arms, or at least not expose one's armpits, whether male or female. For a casual event, pants and blouse would be appropriate for a female.

A national costume is always appropriate.

When in doubt, at any time, by all means telephone your Malay host and enquire.

For a formal Malay function, such as a wedding or business dinner, women guests should wear suitable attire that covers their legs and arms. Ties are not usual for gentlemen — long-sleeved conventional or batik shirts with collars are normally acceptable, as are safari suits.

FORMAL DRESS

If attending an official function, especially in Malaysia, one should be aware that the colour yellow is for Malay royalty. Therefore a commoner should not wear that colour.

ROYAL COLOUR

CONVERSATION

Malays have a gentleness of speech and would never knowingly insult or offend. Modesty is practised when referring to themselves and their families, in an almost deprecating manner.

DEPRECATING SPEECH

Such personal questions as, "How much did it cost?", "What is your salary?" and, "How old are you?" are not intended to be prying, but are commonly asked by Malays and Asians of different ethnic groups. Westerners who find this rude should try to understand and not feel offended.

'PRYING' QUESTIONS

Risque conversation is taboo. Do not

TABOO SUBJECTS

discuss sex, politics or religion. If your Malay host does raise the subject of religion, then you must exercise tact in the conversation.

SAFE SUBJECTS

Complimenting the host's home is a good move as the Malays are a tidy and house-proud people. Sports, particularly football, and movies are also popular topics, along with food and children.

INVITATIONS

VERBAL INVITATION

A personal invitation is often extended by a Malay person rather than a written invitation. Do try your best to accept an invitation that is extended in the form of a personal call. Formal occasions, such as weddings, would call for printed invitations, with no specific preferences for colour.

All invitations, written and personal, must be acknowledged as soon as possible, whether accepting or declining.

THANK YOU

THANK YOU

A verbal thank-you when leaving a function is normally sufficient. A telephone call to your Malay host or hostess the day after the function is also common. Thank-you notes are not normally written and flowers are not normally sent, in the Malay way.

If a small thank-you gift is taken to a home-cooked meal, it would often be in the form of fruit and may be enjoyed by all after the meal.

GIFTS AND OCCASIONS

GENERAL CONSIDERATIONS

Gifts are always a nice thought, but care should be taken not to upset by a poor choice.

Items must be presented with the right hand, supported by the left hand if necessary, in the Malay way.

PRESENTING A GIFT

A gift is not opened in front of the giver. If you receive a present from your Malay friend, express thanks but do not open it in front of the giver.

OPENING A GIFT

Red and green are the colours to choose when selecting wrapping-paper for gifts for Malay friends, red signifying love and green symbolising religion, although other bright colours may also be used.

COLOURS FOR GIFT WRAPPING

Alcohol and cigarettes should never be given to Malays, because their religion forbids consumption of these, nor should ashtrays, wine glasses, knives (they are looked upon as weapons) or personal items such as underclothing and sleepwear.

TABOO GIFTS

A gift of money is always acceptable, whatever the occasion, and is normally

A GIFT OF MONEY

AMOUNT OF
CASH FOR
A GIFT

presented in a green, flowery envelope, with the name of the giver endorsed on the back of the envelope. A white envelope is used when giving money at a funeral.

There is no 'correct' amount, though the amount (in either an odd or even denomination) is usually comparable to the cost of the individual meal provided.

Money may be presented during a *salam* (handshake).

SPECIFIC OCCASIONS AND GIFTS

HOME-COOKED
MEAL

When invited by Malay friends for a home-cooked meal, sweets, fruit (bananas are always appreciated), chocolates and cakes are well thought of. Gifts for the children are always appreciated, especially toys (but not a toy dog or a toy pig since both animals are considered unclean by Muslims).

NEW-BORN BABY

If you are giving a gift on the occasion of a new-born Malay baby, it is usual to give colourful clothing (dresses or jackets) to the infant.

As with some other communities, the new mother and her baby are not encouraged to venture out during the first month after birth (actually 44 days for the Malay community). Visitors are welcome at the home, although early morning and night visits are not favoured.

CIRCUMCISION

Circumcision is compulsory for Muslims. The average age for Malay boys to undergo this is 12 years, after they have completed their reading of the Koran, which they would have studied since young.

Relatives and friends gather together to congratulate the boy, and to enjoy a feast *(kenduri)*. Guests may present money to the boy on this happy occasion. Often the guests will receive beautifully decorated eggs. Appropriate sentiments would be, "Congratulations".

ENGAGEMENT

When attending an engagement party, an appropriate gift, apart from money, would be a length of fabric suitable for making clothing.

The gold engagement ring, often set with diamonds, is worn on the ring finger *(jari manis* or 'sweet finger') of the girl's right hand. Her *fiance* wears a silver ring on the ring finger of his right hand.

MARRIAGE CEREMONY

A marriage ceremony *(akad nikah)* attended by relatives and close friends, is conducted in the presence of a Muslim judge *(kadi)*.

The following day, colourful ceremonies take place with the guests joining in enthusiastically.

A colourful tree-like decoration, *(bunga manggar)* supplied by the bride's family, is placed strategically (perhaps at the corner of the street) to ensure a welcome to the bride's home, especially for the groom. This decoration is very important — the groom may not appear if the decoration is not in evidence!

Upon the arrival of the groom, accompanied by a percussion group, at the bride's home at approximately 2p.m. on the chosen day, he and his bride will pay respects to her relatives at a *bersanding* (sitting-in-state) ceremony. At the ceremony the bride and groom will be feted as a king and queen, seated on a decorated dais *(pelamin)*, while guests admire them.

The couple will then proceed to the groom's home, at approximately 3.30p.m., where they will pay respects to his relatives at a *bertandang* (visiting) ceremony, again seated on a *pelamin* in regal style.

If given some grains of yellow rice, they are for throwing over both shoulders of the bridal pair, as a symbol of good luck. This is done upon the arrival of the groom at the bride's home and then again when the couple leave for the groom's home.

Relatives and close family friends will be invited to either the bride's or the groom's home with the usual time being 11a.m. to 5p.m., incorporating luncheon.

WEDDING
DINNER

Another meal, for other friends, is hosted during the evening, at the bride's home.

SEATING

You should observe what the Malay guests are doing, especially where they sit for the meal, and be guided by them as different families have different customs.

AUSPICIOUS
FARE

Food is generally eaten with the fingers in typical Malay style at such an occasion. Remember to use your right hand. *Nasi*

82

Minyak is usually served at Malay weddings as this rice dish, prepared with yoghurt, onions and garlic, symbolises prosperity.

The wedding gift may be presented at the wedding dinner. An appropriate gift would be a household item such as an iron, fruit juicer or vase, but do remember not to present ashtrays, wine glasses or knives.

After eating, it is usual for guests to wish the bridal couple well with a *salam* (hand shake) at the *bersanding* dais and then place wedding gifts on a special table nearby. Here, one may notice *kain songket*, batik or similar rich fabric folded in elaborate styles. These are gifts of cloth which have been exchanged between the bride and groom. If you are giving money, it is presented during the *salam*, to either the bride or groom, or their parents, and this is called *salam berisi* (hand filled with contents). The bride and groom will gladly accept handshakes, although Muslim guests would not offer their hands to other members of the opposite sex.

Guests may observe that henna (a plant dye) has been used to stain palms, finger nails and toe nails of the newly-married pair, with the stain remaining for about three weeks.

Permission should be obtained before taking photographs at a wedding.

At both *bersanding* and *bertandang* ceremonies, guests are often presented with prettily decorated hard-boiled hens' eggs upon leaving, as a symbol of food, health, wealth and fertility.

BIRTHDAY

For a birthday party, the same etiquette applies pertaining to gifts, dress and eating as for other happy occasions within the Malay community. *Bubur Putih Bubur Merah* is often served. *'Putih'* is 'white' and signifies life, while *'merah'* is 'red' and signifies age. This rice porridge *(bubur)* is cooked with *gula Melaka* (palm sugar) and coconut milk, with the white porridge being served first and the colour porridge, served from the other direction, poured on top of the white porridge. *Pulut Kuning* is equivalent to a birthday cake. This dish is made of glutinous rice cooked with turmeric and topped with beef *rendang* (fried meat curry). Banana leaves, the yellow turmeric rice and beef *rendang* are arranged in layers on a plate and decorated with cucumber, fried onions, tomatoes, carrots and flowers.

HOUSE
WARMING

A housewarming ceremony is often held when a Malay family moves to their new home. A family friend, with a religious background, will lead prayers, after which lunch is usually served. *Briyani* (saffron rice cooked with chicken or mutton) is sometimes featured and there will be plain rice, curry and *sambal* (spicy condiment). A suitable gift would be a household item.

FUNERAL

If confronted with the necessity to attend the funeral of a Malay person, a floral wreath may be sent to the home. Alternatively, you can carry loose flowers, preferably sweet-smelling and in pale colours, and present them to a close family member of the deceased. If you prefer, money may be given to the family, presented in a white envelope with the giver's name endorsed on the back of the envelope.

FLORAL/
MONETARY
CONTRIBUTION

White or sombre colours should be worn when visiting the home to pay your respects.

APPROPRIATE
ATTIRE

After approaching the family of the deceased, it is customary to view the body — simply stand quietly with head bowed.

Burial takes place within 12 hours after death, unless unavoidable.

It is not usual to serve food or drink to visitors, although after the body has left the house drinks (tea) may be served.

Males only proceed to the cemetery.

If you are giving money, it should be presented to a family member when you are leaving the house, with the words, "Let him rest in peace", or similar.

TAKING LEAVE

Persons who enter a mosque, for any reason, must first remove their shoes and leave them neatly at the entrance. Males and females must sit separately, and modest dressing is essential. Women must have their arms and knees covered. It is preferable for all persons to cover their heads. When people are praying, do not walk in front of them. Friday afternoons, from approximately 12 noon until 3 p.m., are busy times as services take place in mosques then.

MOSQUE

Dining Etiquette

PRE-MEAL

Relaxed conversation usually precedes a meal, often with the gentlemen grouped together in the living room and the ladies in the kitchen.

Tea might be served with *kerepek* (a variety of Malay crackers).

SEATING AT THE TABLE

An invitation to a home-cooked meal should be looked forward to, as Malays are very hospitable and enjoy cooking for their guests.

Depending on how traditional your Malay hosts are, you may find yourself seated Western-style, or seated on mats on the floor. Also, the sexes may be segregated, with the men eating first, being served by the women. However, if all eat together as a family then the head of the family will normally sit at the head of the table or mat, with his wife at the other end.

As an honoured guest, you may find yourself at the head of the table or mat, or at the right side of the host. You should wait to be invited to sit.

Females sit together and males do likewise in such a family setting, with the women to the left of the head of the family.

Similar seating arrangements apply in Malay restaurants.

TABLE SETTINGS

In a Malay home, whether seated on colourful mats on the floor or at a table, serving platters of food are placed in the centre, with serving spoons. In both instances, plates are provided for individuals and, traditionally, cutlery is not used unless requested. Malays usually eat with their fingers. | WITH FINGERS

If cutlery is used, then forks will be placed to the left and spoons to the right of individual dinner plates. Knives are not used, as Malay food is served in bite-size portions. The same setting can also be seen in Malay restaurants. | WITH CUTLERY

Rice is eaten with the spoon, with the convex side of the fork used to push the rice on to the spoon. The edge of the spoon may be used to cut pieces of food if there is a need to do so.

Tumblers for water are placed to the top left of each setting. | FOR DRINKS

BREAKFAST, LUNCH AND DINNER

A popular Malay breakfast dish is *Nasi Lemak* (rice cooked with coconut milk, accompa- | BREAKFAST nied by a spicy *sambal* condiment, fish, egg and vegetable). Other favourites are sweet potato and tapioca (either boiled, or fried in a rice flour batter), *Goreng Pisang* (fried banana fritters) and *Pulot Serunding* (glutinous rice with salt).

Tea and coffee are the usual breakfast beverages.

LUNCH

A Malay lunch often consists of rice with fish or meat curry and vegetables. Soya bean curd is a favourite, often served in soup or fried. A chilli-hot condiment called *sambal blachan* is also popular. *Sambal blachan* gives the meal a kick!

Fresh fruit is commonly served as a dessert.

Water is the usual drink with a Malay lunch.

SET MEAL

If you choose a set lunch, or dinner, in a Malay restaurant you will be sure of a representative Malay meal.

For all meals, it will depend on where and what you choose to eat as to the style of service.

STYLE OF
SERVICE

The dishes of food at a Malay meal are generally all served together, in central serving bowls, and each one helps himself or herself. Second helpings may be taken from the serving bowls.

Malay desserts are sweet and rich, and fruit is often offered.

Do check if you are unsure of anything. Your Malay host or the service staff will normally be most happy to enlighten you about their food.

TEA

Tea drinking is an informal affair for Malay people, with friends quite often telephoning to mention they would like to pop in for a social chit-chat.

Tea and coffee are popular with Malays.

The tea leaves used are usually coarse in texture. Pandanus leaves are often added to the tea in the teapot to impart a distinctive flavour. Tea is served with or without milk or sugar, according to guests' preferences.

The coffee is often Malaysian-grown and is really strong. It may be served with or without milk or sugar.

For both drinks, guests are usually asked, when at a Malay home, which way they prefer their tea or coffee, *"Susu?"* (milk), and it is prepared accordingly by the hostess. Evaporated milk or condensed milk is usual.

It is polite to drink at least two cups of tea or coffee, to pay your hostess a compliment on her skills.

Malays are fond of eating snacks during the day. Curry puffs are among their favourite savouries and Goreng Pisang (fried banana fritters) their sweet choice.

Food is eaten in the Malay manner with the right hand and the left hand is used for drinks, although if no food is consumed then the right hand is used for drinks.

PLACING YOUR ORDER

STAPLE FOOD Rice *(nasi)* is always on the menu and is a staple food for Malays.

Ideally, a balance of tastes, textures, colours and aromas should be considered when ordering.

COMPOSITION OF MEAL It is usual to order a chicken or fish dish, one lamb or mutton or beef dish, two vegetable dishes (one with gravy and the other a dry dish) and two side dishes such as *sambal blachan* (a very hot condiment made of chillies, dried shrimp paste and lime juice) and *kropok* (prawn crackers), depending on how many people are eating – remember SHARING FOOD that the dishes are all shared amongst the diners.

Each person helps himself, or herself, from the various central dishes as and when wished throughout the meal.

DESSERT A variety of sweet desserts and cakes is common in Malay cuisine. For examples, see the section on Food, Glorious Food! Fresh fruit is also usually available.

EATING ALONE If you are eating alone, there are set meals and many Malay one-dish meals to choose from.

Popular one-dish meals are *Nasi Goreng* (fried rice), *Soto Ayam* (a substantial soup with shredded chicken, vegetables and cubes of pressed rice), *satay* (barbecued meat on skewers, served with a spicy peanut sauce), *Gado Gado* (salad with a spicy sauce), Chicken curry, *Sayor Loday* (vegetables in coconut gravy) and *Nasi Lemak* (rice cooked with coconut milk, accompanied by fried fish, egg, vegetable and anchovy *sambal*).

There are also noodle dishes such as *Mee Rebus* (yellow noodles with spicy, sweet potato gravy, cubed soya bean curd, green chillies, and hard-boiled egg, garnished with lime) and *Mee Siam* (rice vermicelli with a spicy sauce, cubed soya bean curd, prawns, hard-boiled egg and bean sprouts, garnished with lime).

It should be noted that Muslims only consume food which is certified as *halal* (acceptable) under Islamic law. This means foodstuffs which have been processed, cooked or prepared according to the said law. For instance, meat and poultry must be slaughtered by a Muslim to be *halal*. Any part of a pig and any product derived from that animal are *haram* (forbidden). Liquor and any intoxicating substance are also forbidden. Ducks, frogs and turtles are also not favoured by Muslims.

When you are entertaining Muslim guests, whether at home or in a restaurant, be sure and check beforehand that your choice of food is acceptable, simply by asking your guests. Similarly, as a guest, you should inform your host beforehand of any dietary restrictions you may have. As an act of courtesy to your guests, or hosts, and to make them feel more comfortable, you could refrain from eating prohibited food in their company. You may also wish to forego alcohol.

ORDERING FOOD

If your party is large and informal, you should decide amongst yourselves on which dishes to order, and one person, preferably male, should place the order with the waiter. Alternatively, the host will place the order.

If you do not have a Malay friend to assist you, than ask the waiter for advice on ordering.

For gastronomic delights, see the section on Food, Glorious Food!

ORDERING DRINKS

COLD DRINKS

Water is the usual drink to be served with a Malay meal. After the main course, other drinks may be had. *Bandung* (made with milk and rose syrup) is thought to cool the body after the spiciness of a meal. *Chendol* (based on coconut milk and palm sugar) and fruit juices are popular, as is coconut water.

Beer may be ordered, if desired, in a restaurant (providing it is licensed), but remember that alcohol is forbidden for Muslims to consume.

TEA

Tea, with or without milk or sugar, often ends a Malay meal.

Table Etiquette

As with the Indians, Malay men are seated before women and are also served first.

Muslims offer a short prayer *(doa)*, either publicly or silently, both before and after meals. As a non-Muslim, one need only bow one's head as a mark of respect.

PRAYER

Before eating, it is usual for the Malay host to say, *"Jemput"* (help yourself), to which others will reply with the same word. The host will then say, *"Silakan"* (start now) and so you begin your meal.

INVITATION TO BEGIN

You should wait to be invited by your Malay host to eat and drink initially. To be urged several times shows your politeness in not being greedy.

In the traditional Malay style of eating, food is eaten with the fingers. Hands are therefore always washed before and after meals, whether at home or in a restaurant.

When a Malay host or hostess offers you a small bowl of water and a small towel, they are to be used for the washing and drying of your fingers. Often a teapot-like container,

FINGER BOWL

with a round deep stand, is used for this purpose. The section on SERVIETTES/TABLE NAPKINS will be of help here.

USING FINGERS FOR EATING

The fingers of the right hand must be used for eating purposes, even if you are left-handed.

Using your fingertips, just take a small amount of food and mound it smoothly, then, fingertips facing upwards, put the food quickly into your mouth, using your thumb to push the food in. Try not to spill any food and not to lick your fingers in the process. Take care not to get your palms involved, only your fingertips should be used.

EATING MALAY FOOD WITH A FORK AND SPOON

If it proves really difficult, then request a fork and spoon, remembering to use the spoon for conveying the food to the mouth with the right hand. The fork is used with the concave side of the tines to the diner, to push the food onto the spoon.

Dishes of food are passed around the table from the right to the left.

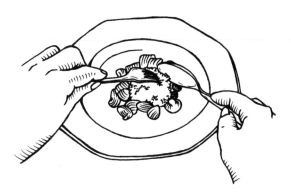

Any food served wrapped in leaves should be opened up properly before beginning eating the meal, otherwise your fingers will become too sticky as the meal progresses, to be able to do the job properly.

FOOD WRAPPED IN LEAVES

You may use your left hand for the passing of dishes and utensils if your right hand is sticky from eating. The loosely clenched fist of your right hand, palm downwards, should support your left arm to show respect in using your right hand.

PASSING SERVING DISHES

If you are eating with a fork and spoon, then use your right hand to pass the serving dishes.

Drinking glasses are also held in the left hand when the right hand is sticky.

When serving yourself from a central serving bowl, use the serving spoon. The common serving spoons must never touch the food on the individual plates, so do take care.

SERVING YOURSELF

Never use your own spoon for this purpose, as it is a major breach of etiquette.

Do not offer food to another person using your own utensils, if used, at any time. Each person should serve himself or herself when food is in central serving bowls.

Rice should be served onto your plate first, and then other food.

The food must be placed on the far (top) side of your plate each time.

Various *sambal* (condiments) are served in small containers with small serving spoons.

CONDIMENTS

Crackers and sliced cucumber are also served. The cool cucumber complements the spicy *sambal*. A favourite condiment is *sambal blachan* made with chillies, dried shrimp paste and lime juice.

If you are eating a meal using your fingers, then cucumber or crackers can be used to scoop the *sambal* on to your plate.

BEGIN BY
EATING RICE

It is the custom to begin a Malay meal by eating one or two mouthfuls of rice first, rice being the principal food. Begin with the rice nearest to you on your plate.

EATING RICE
WITH OTHER
FOOD

The food of your choice on your plate is mixed with the rice nearest to you on your plate, then eaten. Note that the food is mixed with the rice, not the rice with the food.

If only one type of food is tasted in one mouthful, then you can savour the taste of each dish. On the other hand, if you mix small portions of several food types and rice together for one mouthful then you experience a whole kaleidoscope of tastes.

A HOME-
COOKED MEAL

When eating a home-cooked Malay meal, serve yourself small portions from three or four dishes at first so that you can have second helpings later. To only eat one helping is considered disrespectful to your hosts. To have seconds is to compliment the hostess.

An observant Malay host will ask a guest to take more food, particularly rice, before the guest has finished eating all his food.

FINISHING
A MEAL

It is good etiquette at a Malay meal to

finish eating all the rice on one's plate, although it is good manners to leave a little other food or drink unfinished.

Upon finishing a Malay meal with a Western setting, the fork and spoon are placed side by side on the individual dinner plate, with the two handles towards the diner.

UTENSILS

After a meal it is customary to say, *"Terima kasih"* (thank you) to your host and the host will reply with, *"Sama-sama"* (same to you) and the host will also say, *"Syukur"* (thanks to God). Then a short prayer is said by the host and his family.

It is not customary to take one's leave immediately after a meal in a Malay home, but rather to stay a short time engaging in conversation before departing. This is important in the Malay way.

TAKING LEAVE AFTER A MEAL

SPECIFIC MALAY FOOD

Satay, a firm favourite amongst Malays, is meat (beef, mutton or chicken) marinated in a spicy mixture, threaded on skewers and barbecued. The sticks of cooked *satay* are dipped in spicy peanut sauce before being eaten with sliced cucumber, raw onion and *ketupat* (a square piece of steamed rice cake wrapped in coconut leaves).

SATAY

The spicy peanut sauce is served either in a central bowl or in small individual bowls. If the former, you may request some small bowls and distribute the sauce before beginning eating, or use a spoon and transfer the sauce to individual plates. It is not proper, when eating with Muslims, to intimately share food (including sauces) from common receptacles.

If the meat on a stick of *satay* is too much to be eaten in one mouthful, the remaining meat after the first bite can be pushed to the tip of the stick by using a fork or the edge of your individual sauce bowl. If an individual sauce bowl is not available, bite the meat and slide the skewer off without putting the end of the skewer in your mouth.

KETUPAT

Ketupat (in a small packet made of coconut leaves) is usually served cut in halves, with the rice pre-cut into small squares. The packet must be opened neatly and completely before commencing eating, with the rice remaining on the leaves. Fingers are used to open the *ketupat* packet.

The *ketupat*, onion and cucumber are eaten by using the *satay* sticks as skewers. Pierce the individual pre-cut squares of *ketupat* and dip into the peanut sauce a cube at a time.

The leaves from the *ketupat* must be placed neatly on a plate upon finishing.

Satay sticks, when finished with, must be placed neatly to one side of the serving plate, or, if there is insufficient space to do so hygienically, another plate should be used for this purpose. This is done because individual plates are not usually served to diners when eating *satay*. However if you are served with an individual plate then it will be used for this purpose. Discarded *satay* sticks are never placed directly on the table in the Malay way of etiquette.

SOUP

At a Malay meal, soup is served in one central soup tureen, with a soup ladle.

Consumed throughout the meal, soup is for moistening the rice and not only for drinking's sake. You simply take a little soup stock from the tureen, using the soup ladle, and gently pour it on the rice on your own plate.

Solid soup ingredients are removed from the central tureen, using the soup ladle, and placed neatly on your own plate, to the far (top) side.

If by chance you are served with a small individual bowl of soup, the same etiquette applies as for the central soup tureen, and you will be given a soup spoon. The soup spoon is therefore used to spoon the liquid over your rice, and for the taking of solid ingredients.

The left hand will be used for this purpose, as the right hand will be sticky from eating.

If you are using a soup spoon, the spoon remains in the individual soup bowl upon finishing, with the spoon handle towards the diner.

BONES

Malays display *finesse* with their eating habits and this applies all the way down the line to bones and other inedible matter.

All discarded bones must be placed by the diner neatly in the same direction on the top (far) side of the individual plate. To do otherwise shows a lack of breeding in Malay etiquette.

No food or inedible matter is placed on the table when eating Malay style. To do so is a breach of basic food etiquette.

When eating meat from a bone, the bone remains on the plate and the fingers of the right hand are used to pick the meat off the bone.

At the end of a Malay meal, any left-overs on the individual plate should be pushed to the centre of the plate, neatly.

SERVIETTES/TABLE NAPKINS

Serviettes or table napkins, as such, are not always available when eating Malay style.

If a serviette or table napkin is provided, it should be kept on the diner's lap except when being used to gently wipe hands and mouth. After the meal, the soiled section should be folded inwards and the serviette folded neatly and placed on the table next to your setting.

In a home-setting there will always be a finger bowl on the table for use both before and after eating.

Often a teapot-like container, with a round, deep stand, is used. The host will pour water from the container over the guests' fingers, using the stand to collect the waste water.

Drying of the fingers is done slowly and gently on the towel provided. The used section of the towel is folded inwards and the towel is placed neatly at the side of the finger bowl.

When having snacks or tea, small finger bowls will be placed upon the table, with an attractively arranged hand-towel placed under the bowl, on the saucer. After dipping the fingers into the small bowl of water, gently and slowly dab the fingers dry on the edge of the towel.

BUFFET

Malay meals are not traditionally served buffet style. When a Malay or Indonesian meal is presented in such a style, it is approached in the same manner as for a Western buffet meal. This means helping yourself, throughout the meal, from a long table laden with food and returning to your own table to eat. Numerous small helpings should be taken.

When helping yourself, take the food nearest to you, both from the serving container and from the buffet table, using the cutlery provided. Do not dig in the centre but slowly scoop the food, whether it be from the side or front of the container. To do otherwise is considered impolite.

Always keep the food in the containers looking neat. This is very important in the Malay style of etiquette.

It is ill-mannered to lean across another person when helping yourself to food.

BUSINESS

The same 'rules' apply to invitations, dress and the giving and receiving of business cards, as with most other Asian societies.

Never assume that a spouse is included in an invitation, check with the office concerned if you are unsure.

When giving and receiving a business card, two hands must be used. The card is handed over so that the recipient can read it as given to him. A bow, or nod of the head, indicates good business etiquette when giving and receiving cards.

Business is not discussed until after pleasantries have been disposed of, in fact, sometimes never at all.

If the business function is in a restaurant, it should be one that the host is familiar with, and the menu should be chosen in advance in order that the host appears well-prepared and no problem arises.

Festive Fare

Hari Raya Puasa, at the end of the month-long fast of *Ramadan*, is celebrated joyously by Muslims on the tenth month of the Islamic calendar — usually depending on the sighting of the new moon.

HARI RAYA PUASA

The tenth month of the Islamic calendar is called *Syawal*, and it varies greatly from the Gregorian calendar.

Fasting, from approximately 5 a.m. until approximately 7 p.m. daily, is an act of penance. By observing *Ramadan*, Muslims are reminded of the suffering of others. Most importantly, each individual Muslim will go through the experience of self-restraint. It is a period of spiritual enhancement. All able-bodied Muslims adhere to the abstinence of eating and drinking from dawn until dusk during this solemn and important holy month. Reading of the Koran and praying are required. *Fitrah* (monetary donations) are given to mosques by all Muslims, to be used to assist the less fortunate.

FASTING MONTH

Seven days before Hari Raya Puasa, at

night, *Malam Tujoh Leko* (seven night countdown) begins. Muslim households switch on decorative lighting, turning on more lights each night until, on the eve of the festival, the full complement is alight in a colourful blaze.

DECORATIONS

Homes will be at their very best, with new colourful table-cloths, cushions and other household items, for the occasion.

ATTIRE

Colourful clothing will be worn for Hari Raya Puasa and it is the time of year when males wear beautiful *kain samping* (short, gold-threaded sarong worn over trousers and shirt) and *songkok* (dark, velvet cap). Females wear lovely *baju kurong* (ankle-length dress) and *selendang* (head scarf).

The first day of Hari Raya Puasa is a celebration for accomplishing the fasting month, and of thankfulness. Prayers are said at mosques or in open fields, and family ties are strengthened by visiting homes of relatives.

FESTIVE FARE

Hari Raya Puasa is the time to enjoy eating traditional delicacies such as *Kueh Lopis* (glutinous rice cake covered with coconut and sugar), *Kueh Dodol* (a coconut based sweet), *Sambal Goreng* (prawns, beef, soya bean curd, long beans and spices cooked in coconut milk), *Sayor Loday* (vegetable-stew in coconut gravy), *Sambal Udang* (prawns cooked in a spicy paste), *satay*, curries, *rendang* (fried meat curry) and *ketupat*.

Ketupat is a symbol of prosperity because the Malays are, traditionally, rice planters. Therefore, the rice-cake is a luxury to indicate that the paddy field is well harvested. *Ketupat* is a 'must' for Hari Raya Puasa. On this festive occasion it is eaten with *rendang*.

Soft drinks and fruit juices are the usual beverages.

As a guest, it is courteous to accept and partake of food and drink on such an important occasion.

FESTIVE GIFT

A gift of a bouquet of flowers (especially roses, a symbol of love and beauty), or sweets, or fruit, though not necessary, would be appreciated by the host family when you are a guest at a Hari Raya Puasa feast.

MONETARY GIFT

Children enjoy receiving *zakat* (gifts of money) from relatives and friends. The money is presented in a decorative envelope during a *salam* (handshake). The amount is at the discretion of the giver and usually ranges between $1 and $10.

SPOKEN GREETING

The usual greeting is, *"Selamat Hari Raya"* (peaceful Hari Raya, or, peaceful celebration day).

HARI RAYA HAJI

Another festival observed by Muslims, and not to be confused with Hari Raya Puasa, is Hari Raya Haji which falls on the tenth day of the twelfth month of the Muslim calendar.

The twelfth month of the Islamic calendar is called *Dzulhijjah*. Hari Raya Haji is therefore observed after Hari Raya Puasa.

Hari Raya Haji commemorates the *Haj* (pilgrimage) to Mecca by Muslims in fulfilment of part of their religious obligations.

Those Muslims who have performed the *Haj* will wear traditional white clothing on this occasion, including white skull caps for males and white head-coverings for females.

Fasting is encouraged on the eve of Hari Raya Haji.

On the day itself, after morning prayers, sheep, cattle and goats are slaughtered at mosques and religious centres in remembrance of the willingness of the prophet Abraham to sacrifice his son, Ismail, to fulfil Allah's will. Allah finally commanded that a sheep be sacrificed instead. The slaughtered animals are shared amongst the community.

New household articles that were in evidence at the earlier festival of Hari Raya Puasa will be utilised again for Hari Raya Haji, and the same type of food will also be prepared.

Hari Raya Haji is a day of family prayers, when family members visit their elders who have previously performed the *Haj.*

If you visit a Muslim household on this occasion, you could present sweets or fruit, although a gift is not necessary.

The usual greeting is *"Selamat Hari Raya"* (peaceful celebration day).

Food, Glorious Food!

Rice *(nasi)* is the principal food in a Malay meal.

STAPLE FOOD

Malay cuisine features coconut, chilli and spices with meat, chicken, fish and vegetables, among other foods.

You can freshen your taste buds with tastes that range from chilli-hot to sweet and sour to cool and sweet.

The Malay style of cooking is similar to some Indonesian dishes.

No Malay meal would be complete without *sambal blachan*. This chilli-hot condiment is made with fresh chillies, dried shrimp paste and lime juice. Powerful!

SAMBAL BLACHAN

Satay is, arguably, the most famous and popular Malay dish. This is mentioned in detail on pages 97 and 98.

SATAY

Nasi Padang is a meal of curried meat, poultry, seafood and vegetables served with rice – it is spicy hot and coconut milk is used in the cooking. *'Nasi'* means 'rice', and Padang is a city in Sumatra, Indonesia, from where this style of cooking evolved.

NASI PADANG

You select your choice of dishes from pre-cooked food displayed prominently in *Nasi Padang* restaurants, and share amongst your party. The section on PLACING YOUR ORDER in this book will be of help in choosing dishes for this type of meal.

Depending on the restaurant, you either help yourself to the food on display, or serving staff will serve you from trays brought to your table.

RIJSTAFFEL

Rijstaffel (Dutch for 'rice table') is less spicy than *Nasi Padang*. Developed during the Dutch colonial era, this is an elaborate meal of Indonesian dishes. Rice is accompanied by a large variety of side dishes such as spicy fish, meat, poultry, egg, nuts, fruit and pickles, of different tastes and texture.

OTHER FAVOURITES

Other Malay favourites include *Soto Ayam* (*'ayam'* is chicken), which is a clear chicken soup with a spicy taste, and *Ayam Goreng* (fried chicken). *Tahu Goreng* (*'tahu'* is soft soya bean curd and *'goreng'* means fried), is a nutritious dish served with a spicy sauce. *Rendang* is a dry meat curry with coconut milk and hot spices. *Sayor Loday* is vegetables in coconut gravy, and *Rojak*, a Malay-style salad served with a spicy sauce. *Kangkong Goreng* is a fried green leafy vegetable with chilli, and this dish is eaten often as it is considered to be cooling to the body. Other popular dishes are *Nasi Goreng* (fried rice) and *Mee Goreng* (fried noodles).

DESSERT

For dessert, *Goreng Pisang* is a firm

favourite of fried banana fritters served hot. You may like to try *agar-agar*, a jelly made of seaweed, or *gula Melaka* which is a cold sago pudding prepared with palm sugar syrup and coconut milk, or one of the many varieties of delicious *kueh* (cake) with coconut milk and rice flour as the main ingredients.

"Jemput."
Help yourself!

INDEX

Adab (Malay manners) 67
Aippasi (seventh lunar month of
    Hindu calendar) 59

Baby, new-born
    Indian 28
    Malay 80
Baju kurong (traditional Malay
    dress) 74, 104
Banana leaf 38-39, 41, 43, 50-52, 53
Beckoning
    Indian style of 19
    Malay style of 73
Beliefs
    Indian 11
    Malay *See* Islam
Bersanding (sitting-in-state by bride
    and groom at a Malay wedding)
    82-83
Bertandang (visiting ceremony at a
    Malay wedding) 82, 83
Bindi (red paste) 29
Birthday
    Indian 34
    Malay 84
Body-touching
    Indian attitude towards 18-19
    Malay attitude towards 72
Bones and other inedible matter
    Indian treatment 56
        eating meat from a bone 56
    Malay treatment 98-99, 100
        eating meat from a bone 100

Bread
    Indian 41, 42, 63
    eating bread 52
Breakfast
    Indian 40
    Malay 87-88
Buffet
    Indian style 57-58
    Malay style 101-102
Bunga manggar (decoration at a
    Malay wedding) 81
Business
    Indian 58, 60
    Malay 102

Calendar,
    Hindu 12
    Muslim 67
    Sikh 12
Cats 17
Choli (Indian blouse) 20
Coffee 42, 89
Colours
    Indian preference
        dress 24
        gift wrapping 26
        pottu 21
        turbans 20-21
    Malay preference
        dress 74
        gift wrapping 79
        royal colour 75
Condiments

Indian 49-50
Malay 95-96
Conversation
  with Indians 24-25
  with Malays 75-78
Cutlery, use of
  with Indian food 49
  with Malay food 87, 94

Deepavali Festival 59-61
  attire 60
  decoration 59
  festive fare 60-61
  festive gift 61
  greeting 61
  monetary gift 61
Dessert
  Indian 41, 52-53, 60, 63-64
  Malay 90, 108-109
Dhoti (Indian attire) 20
Dietary restrictions
  Indian 44-45
  Muslim
    halal (acceptable) 91
    haram (forbidden) 91
Doa See Prayer
Dogs 17, 71
Dress
  Indian
    colours 24
    formal dress 24
    modest dressing 24, 36
    traditional dress 20-24
  Malay
    colours 74
    formal dress 75
    taboos 74-75
    traditional dress 74, 76-77
Drinks
  Indian preference 37, 46
  Malay preference 92
Dupatta (Indian scarf) 20
Dzulhijjah (twelfth month of
  Islamic calender) 105

Engagement
  Indian 28

Malay 81

Farewell
  Indian way 19
  Malay way 73
Fasting, by Muslims 103, 106
Festivals
  Indian
    Deepavali 59-61
  Malay
    Hari Raya Haji 105-106
    Hari Raya Puasa 103-105
Finger bowl
  Indian 47-48, 57
  Malay 101
Fingers, use of for eating
  Indian way 48, 53
  Malay way 87, 89, 94
Fish head curry 54-55
Flowers
  Indian
    funeral 27, 35
    garland 27
    preference 26-27
    wedding 29-30
  Malay
    funeral 84-85
    preference 105
Funeral
  Indian 35
    attire 35
    floral contribution 27, 35
    monetary contribution 27, 35
    taking leave 35
  Malay 84-85
    attire 85
    floral contribution 85
    monetary contribution 85
    taking leave 85

Garland, presenting a 27
Ghee 50
Gifts
  for Indians 26-28
    birthday 34
    colours for wrapping 26
    Deepavali Festival 61

engagement 28
home-cooked meal 28
housewarming 34
monetary gift 27-28, 61
new-born baby 28
presenting and opening a gift 26
taboo gifts 26
wedding gift 28, 31
for Malays 79-81, 83
birthday 84
circumcision 81
colours for gift wrapping 79
engagement 81
Hari Raya Haji 106
Hari Raya Puasa 105
home-cooked meal 78, 80
housewarming 84
monetary gift 79-80, 105
new-born baby 80
presenting and opening a gift 79
taboo gifts 79, 80
wedding gift 83
Giving and receiving an item
Indian 18
Malay 72
Greetings
Indian 13
Malay 67-68
Gurdwara (Sikh place of worship)
12, 35-36

Haj (Muslim Pilgrimage) 106
Haji (prefix to male Muslim Name)
69
*Hajjah (prefix to female Muslim
name)* 69
Halal See Dietary restrictions
Hands, use of
Indian way 18, 42
Malay way 72, 89
Handshake
with Indians 13
with Muslims 68
Haram See Dietary restrictions
Hari Raya Haji 105-106
attire 106
decoration 106

festive fare 106
festive gift 106
greeting 106
pligrimage 106
Hari Raya Puasa 103-105
attire 104
decoration 104
festive fare 104-105
festive gift 105
greeting 105
monetary gift 105
Hinduism 11-12
Holy ash, Hindu *(viboothi)* 21, 24
Home, visiting an Indian
decor 15-17
farewell 19
first visit 17
Hindu 15-16
Muslim 17
removal of shoes 15
seating 18
Sikh 16-17
Home, visiting a Malay
dos and don'ts 70
farewell 73
prayer items 70
prayer times 70-71
removal of shoes 70
seating 71
Housewarming
Hindu 34
Malay 84
Sikh 34-35

Indian community 11
Indian food *See* Indian Muslim
food, North Indian food, Sikh
food, South Indian food,
Vegetarian Indian food
Indian Muslim food 107-108
briyani (saffron rice) 63
Halwa (dessert) 64
roti paratha (bread) 63
Indonesian food
Nasi Padang 107-108
Rijstaffel 108
Introductions

Indian 14-15
Malay 69-70
Invitations
Indian 25
Malay 78
Islam 67

Kacch (Sikh special underwear) 12
Kadi (Muslim judge) 81
Kain samping (short gold-threaded
sarong) 104
Kangha (Sikh comb) 12
Kara (Sikh steel bracelet) 12
Kenduri (Malay feast) 81
Kesa (Sikh uncut, unshaven hair)
12
Ketupat (rice cake) 98, 104, 105
Khanda (Sikh symbol) 16-17
Kirpan (Sikh double-edged sword)
12
Koran (Islamic holy book) 17, 70,
81, 103

Leaves, food wrapped in 50, 95
Lunch
Indian 40
Malay 88

Malay community 67
Malay food 82-84, 86, 89-92, 97-98,
104-105, 107-109
see also Indonesian food
Marriage *See* Wedding
Masala tea 42
Meal, composition of
Indian 43
Indian vegetarian 45
Malay 90
Mitti (Indian toe ring) 29
Mosque 85
Muslim prayer items 17, 70

Names
Indian 14
Malay 68-69
Nasi Padang (Indonesian food)
107-108

North Indian food 31, 33, 37, 42-43,
60-64
Numerology
Indian 27-28
Malay 80

One-dish meals
Indian 43-44
Malay 90-91
Ordering food and drink
Indian style 43-44, 45, 46
Malay style 90, 91-92

Paan (digestive) 53-54
Pallu (Sikh wedding scarf) 32
Passing in front of someone
Indian way 19
Malay way 73
Passing serving dishes
Indian way 49
Malay way 94
Pelamin (Malay marriage dais) 82
Pilgrimage *See Haj*
Pointing
Indian style 19
Malay style 72-73
Pottu (dot on forehead of Indian
women) 21
Prayer at meals
Indian 47
Malay *(doa)* 93, 97
Muslim prayer times 70-71

Ramadan (Muslim fasting month)
103
Rangoli (Indian decoration) 16
Rice
Indian 41, 42
eating rice with other food 52
Malay 96
eating rice with other food 96
Rijstaffel (Indonesian food) 108

Salam (Malay greeting) 68, 83
Salwar-kamez (traditional Indian
dress) 20
Sambal blachan (condiment) 107

Sari (traditional Indian dress) 20
Satay 97-99
Seating
  Indian style
    at home 18
    in a restaurant 38
    at the table 37-38
    at a wedding ceremony 30, 32
    at a wedding reception 31, 33, 34
  Malay style
    at home 71
    in restaurant 87
    at the table 86-87
    at a wedding 82
Selendang (Malay scarf) 104
Serviette *See* Table napkin
Serving yourself
  Indian style 49
  Malay style 88
Set meal
  Indian 41
  Malay 88
Sharing food
  Indian way 43, 45
  Malay way 90
Shoes, removal of
  in Indian homes 15
  in Indian temples 35-36
  in Malay homes 70
  in mosques 85
Sikh food 62, 64
Sikh temple *See Gurdwara*
Sikhism 12
Smoking 18, 72
Snacks
  Indian 37, 42
  Malay 86, 89
Songkok (Malay Cap) 104
Soup
  Indian 55-56
  Malay 99
South Indian food 33, 34, 37, 42-44, 46, 54-55, 62, 63
Sri Guru Granth Sahib (Sikh holy book) 17, 32, 34-35
Staple food

  Indian 42
  Malay 90
Style of service
  Indian
    banana leaf 50-52
    thali 38, 41
  Malay 88
Syawal (tenth month of Muslim calendar) 103

Table etiquette
  Indian
    commencing to eat 51-52
    finger bowl 57
    fingers, use of for eating 48
    finishing a meal 53
    guest-of-honour to begin 47
    home-cooked meal 53
    indicating thanks after a meal 54
    invitation to begin eating 47
    passing serving dishes 49
    serving yourself 49
    sharing food 43
    taking leave after a meal 54
  Malay
    commencing to eat 96
    finger bowl 100-101
    fingers, use of for eating 94
    finishing a meal 96-97
    home-cooked meal 96
    indicating thanks after a meal 97
    invitation to begin eating 93
    passing serving dishes 94, 95
    serving yourself 95
    taking leave after a meal 97
Table Napkins
  Indian 53, 56-57
  Malay 100
Table settings
  Indian style
    with banana leaf 38-39
    with cutlery 39-40
    for drinks 40
    with *thali* 38
  Malay style
    with cutlery 87
    for drinks 87

with fingers 87

Tea
   Indian 41-42
   Malay 89
Temple, Indian 35-36
Thali (marriage necklace) 29
Thali (tray) 38, 53
Thank you
   Indian 25
   Malay 78
Turban 20-21

Vegetarian Indian Food 45, 63
Visiting
   an Indian home 15-17
   a Muslim home 17
   a Sikh home 16-17

Wedding
   Hindu 29-31
      arrival of guests 29-30
      attire 24
      auspicious fare 31
      decoration 30
      gift, choosing 28
      presenting the wedding gift 29, 31
      reception 31
      ritual 30-31
      seating 30, 31
   Malay *(akad nikah)* 81-84
      attire 74, 75
      auspicious fare 82-83
      bersanding 82-84
      bertandang 82-84
      decoration 81
      presenting the wedding gift 83
      reception 82
      ritual 81, 82-84
      seating 82
   Sikh 31-34
      arrival of guests 31-32
      attire 24, 31
      auspicious fare 33
      gift choosing 28
      presenting the wedding gift 32
      reception 33-34

ritual 32-33
seating 32, 33-34

Zakat (gift of money) 105